Why is There a Man And He's Not Mine?

My dear, sweet Christa,

It was a delight to have met you! May God honor your hearts desires & answer all your prayers! God bless you & may He embrace You in His sweet love!

Orpah
2/9/16

Orpah Omega Lee
C. Marasigan

Edited by Leslie Lofranco-Berbano and Ammi Belle M.Armas

Designed and Illustrated by Aurora Morealis

Why is There a Man and He's Not Mine?

Edited by Leslie Lofranco-Berbano and Ammi Belle M.Armas
Designed and Illustrated by Aurora Morealis
www.aurora.morealis.com

G12 GLOBAL DESIGN, INC.
Strategic Communications
Ortigas Center, Pasig City 1605
Telephone: (632) 6872236 to 37
Telefax: (632) 6378248
Email: g12.publish@gmail.com

First Printing, 2013
Printed in the Philippines
ISBN: 978-971-95793-0-4

Ordering Information:
Quantity sales. Special discounts are available on quantity purchases by churches, corporations, associations, and others. For details, contact the publisher at the address above or visit or call the Philippine Campus Crusade for Christ Bookstore at (632) 412-5428 or (632) 412-5429. Address at #40 Scout Borromeo St. South Triangle Homes Quezon City, Philippines1103.

To my two beautiful nieces,
Camille Ruth and Hesed Faith

What People Are Saying About "Why is There a Man and He's Not Mine?"

Orpah listened to most of my longings as a single female. She journeyed with me as I allowed my heart to be vulnerable first to God and then to my husband Anthony. She helped shape my deep foundation in Jesus Christ, to draw from Him as my source of life rather than from a partner or spouse to complete me.

I have gotten to know Orpah deeper through this book, with the realization that He can fill all the gaps in our lives, if we let Him. She just has so much to offer in relationships.

This book allows you to be in touch with your longings and desires that need not be hidden. A must-read.

Maricel Laxa-Pangilinan, wife, mother, actress, host, speaker, author, columnist, publisher, triathlete

This is a very delightful, daring, courageous and inspiring book that both charms the readers with her lively, vivid stories while encouraging them through her experiences of God's goodness and faithfulness. The author also engages single women toward personal reflection and write a letter to God through "Journaling My Thoughts" at the end of each chapter.

I highly recommend this book which points the readers to God, the source of the author's delight, redemption and strength especially during tough times. It challenged me as a pastor to ask forgiveness from every single adult lady whom I fail to pray for, encourage and serve in her journey of faith. Pastors would start doing a great service by being sensitive and understanding to single women, and by leading them to read this book.

Indeed, as Orpah herself said, if she had gotten married, we would not have the benefit of reading this heart-moving book. But as her pastor-friend, I will pray that God would grant her the blessing of a Life-partner, and maybe a sequel can be written, "There is a Man, and He's Mine!"

Dr. Nomer Bernardino, Senior Pastor of Bread From Heaven Community Church, author, speaker

Refreshingly candid and honest, Orpah creatively chronicles her journey through the ups and downs of being a Christian single woman, and how by God's grace, she has grown through them. Single women of all ages will relate to the legitimate longings and struggles she shares, especially the unrequited desire to have a husband who loves her and children to care for.

As she invites the reader to journey with her through her aches and joys, she also shares the beautiful benefits of living unencumbered for the Lord, thus maximizing life for Him.

Truly this hilariously funny but also tearjerker of a book will touch the hearts not only of single women, but all women, and give them hope for a full and meaningful life.

Deonna Tan-Chi, wife of Peter Tan-Chi, Founder and Senior Pastor of the Christ's Commission Fellowship

Orpah has been my friend for more than two decades. We walked closely together as sisters in ministry during my years living in the Philippines and have maintained our friendship from afar since. Orpah has admirably lived what she writes in this book...yes, the ache for a companion has been present and vulnerably acknowledged AND she has lived a rich, full, meaningful, whole life even with an unfulfilled longing in her heart. She walks with integrity what she has written herein. Whether single or married, you will be as blessed and informed by her writing as I am by her life.

Connie Blake, M.A., Director of Debriefing and Renewal (DAR) / Consultation on DAR at Mission Training International, Colorado, USA

Although it is an easy and enjoyable read, this book touches on very serious life matters. Orpah's candid honesty and openness in sharing her truest and deepest thoughts, feelings and experiences makes it impossible not to realize the presence of longings within our single friends and become more sensitive to them. And even if the book centers on the many faces of single blessedness, there is much to relate to even for married persons such as myself. Most importantly, it speaks of maturity, acceptance, faith, love, wisdom, appreciation and an amazing zest for life.

Mikee Cojuangco-Jaworski, Philippine equestrienne, Gold medalist in the 2002 Asian Games in Busan, South Korea; International Olympic Committee member 2013; actress, TV host, public servant

Contents

To all my friends who took me into their homes, loved and fed me when I started writing this book:
Angie and Rey Luciano in Sydney;
Suwanna Akrapongpisak in Bangkok;
Ruth Abesamis in Michigan;
and Ching Dayot in Makiling, Laguna

To the editors in my family:
Mrs. Elayda C. Marasigan,
Daniel Lee Darwin,
Leah Ruth Marasigan-Darwin, and
Ammi Belle Marasigan-Armas

To my wonderful, real editors Leslie Lofranco-Berbano and Ammi Belle Marasigan-Armas

To Dr. Philip Gordon Ney, and George and Connie Blake, my counseling mentors who first helped me in my journey of rediscovering God's design for me

To Rory for her great ideas and fun illustrations

To my crazy and fun Marasigan family

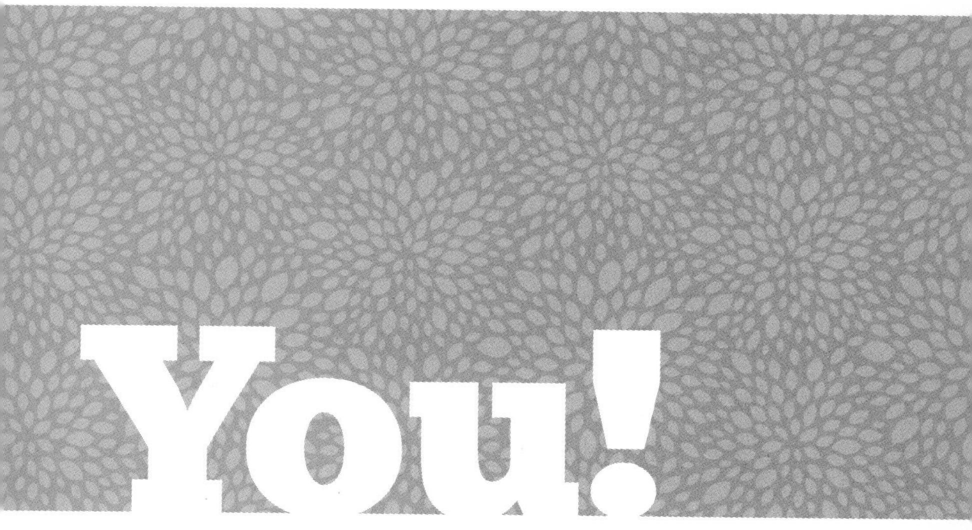

To Joe who always asked me,
"How's your book? Is it done?"
Well, here it is, Joe!

To Chevy Morales and Noemi Maano, who helped in the initial editing, and the young ladies who first tested my book and knew it would work even for them
–Faith, Bea, Pristine, and Janina

To my Philippine Campus Crusade for Christ family who encouraged me to write and eagerly expected me to finish this book so that they could give it to their single friends

And to the Author of my Single Life, the sweet Lover of my soul,
Jesus Christ
Thank you for my story!

Preface

Single, never-married, beautiful, godly women. There are still so many of these lovely creations of God walking around planet Earth. Why aren't they all taken in marriage?

Men. What is our experience of them? In all our stories as women, there have been men who either nurtured us and made us blossom, or deeply damaged our hearts.

Not many people understand my conflicts as a single woman. Many people have left me wondering because usually they would tell me:

- ★ I'm not being as spiritual as I should be – that's why I'm single;
- ★ The problem lies within my personality (i.e. I'm not "soft or feminine enough" or I'm "too strong" for a woman) – that's why I'm single;
- ★ I'm too busy – that's why I'm single;
- ★ I'm focusing too much on my being single – that's why I'm single.

This book is dedicated to all the single never-married women like me who try to live well in a world of married people. No one, in my experience, has courageously spoken about the difficulties of living as a single woman who also sincerely wants to love and obey God.

How difficult is it for a single woman who longs for deep connections with both men and women to be able to give her heart in relationships? Can a single woman come away from these same relationships still in tune with herself? Can she hope that all the joys, frustrations and disappointments she experiences will drive her to God Who alone can satisfy her deepest longings?

How can I, as a single woman, have an amazing impact on the lives of people? How do I deal with the in-your-face triggers that remind me that I have no husband to come home to; no children to enjoy and take care of; and no one to grow old with? The truth is, I may grow old alone and die in my single bed.

I am sure many single women have had thoughts like mine, and tend to push them away instead of facing them head-on. It takes a lot of courage to say all these out loud. But it's about time that somebody did. So say them out loud I did in this book, and I hope you will join me as you read on.

This book is about my journey as a single woman of at least 50 years who intends not only to survive, but more important, to live her single life well. It is unabashedly Christian in intent. Through it, I hope to share with you what my experience has been as I try to live an authentic, passionate, single woman's life in a world that may not give us all the things we want. My hope is that my story will encourage you, teach you, and make you think of your own life and the way you relate to others, especially to men.

All the anecdotes, events, organizations and the names of my family members are true but some names of individuals, such as the names of my male and female friends as well as places I have been to, have been changed to protect their identity. I have written this book in a span of more than one year in five different countries: Australia, Canada, Philippines, Thailand and the USA, eating amazing food from each country with wonderful loving hosts who allowed me to write in the comfort of their homes. To all these friends, I am deeply grateful.

At the end of each chapter of this book are questions and activities that might help as you think about your own life. You may use this section, "Journaling My Thoughts," to personally reflect on your own journey as a single person. I encourage you to write down your thoughts and turn them into a prayer to God. You never know when God's Spirit moves and our hearts well up with so many things to say to Him. So do have a pen ready when you sit down to read this book!

You may also use these questions for discussions with the women you mentor or lead in Bible Studies. If you are married, this book might help you understand and minister to single women. If so, bless your single friends with a gift of this book. If you are a man, this may help you know more about us women and show you how best to minister to us.

To all of you single women, my hope is that wherever you are in your journey of singleness, this book will remind you that there is deep joy and fulfillment in being a single woman. May our hearts be full of joy in knowing that, whether God sees it fit for us to have a husband or not, we will be the best single ladies we can be, loving and helping others for God's glory, with hearts that are fully alive to God.

Orpah Omega Lee C. Marasigan

February 14, 2012

Why is There a Man And He's Not Mine?

CHAPTER ONE

1 Why is There a Man And He's Not Mine?

I lived on a beautiful mountain in British Columbia, Canada from February until September 2004. It was my sabbatical leave from my work as a missionary with Campus Crusade for Christ. A friend of mine, whom I shall call William, invited me to stay there with his family for as long as I wanted that year. William and his wife Ann own a lovely estate situated on acres of land atop a small mountain with a 360-degree view of forests, ocean, and snow-capped peaks. They have a special name for their mountain, but for purposes of this story, I shall call their mountain, Montagne d'amour, or the Love Mountain. When visitors come to their mountain, William and Ann lovingly offer them a quiet retreat that ministers to their bodies and souls. William allowed me to stay in one of his four houses on the mountain. He let me use his old van and gave me the privilege of exploring his mountain. Because I was a city girl, the mountain was both scary and exciting. It took me about a month before I got used to walking around.

I woke up to the view of the Strait of San Juan de Fuqua, which separates Washington and Canada. There were hummingbirds flying outside my window and sometimes woodpeckers pecked away on the distant trees. This mountain was so high that sometimes, when I looked down, I would see an eagle soaring below. I would walk up and down the mountain for about one and a half kilometers each way almost every day, which helped me become so fit by the time I left Montagne d'amour.

My temperament is sanguine, which means I usually come alive when I have someone to interact with and relate to. So you can imagine that it was quite a challenge for me to live alone on that mountain. It was very lonely living alone, at least for the first few weeks.

Diego, My Canine Companion

William allowed me to adopt and take care of his half-wolf, half-German Shepherd dog, Diego. I would go on walks almost every day with Diego. As he accompanied me, he would first walk ahead of me to make sure there were no cougars crossing our path. Then he would come back to my side to tell me it was safe. I would have my quiet reading and worship times in the beautiful meadows. Sometimes I needed to climb up some big rocks. I would hang on to poor old Diego and he would willingly sit still until I managed to pull myself up. In the deeper parts of the mountain, I would sing at the top of my lungs with Diego as the only member of my appreciative audience.

For a few weeks, having a canine companion seemed much better than having no companion at all, and yet, because I was designed by God to relate to the human species, somehow Diego's love and attention lacked something. I felt I needed another human being to relate to!

During that first month, one of William's friends came to visit him on the mountain. He was a single, blue-eyed Irish man who would say "Top-o'-the morning to Ya" as I imagined all Irish men would say which means "Good Morning!" in Irish slang. He asked William if he could stay temporarily in that place while he looked for an apartment in the city. He occupied a loft in one of William's other houses. He was going to be around for a few weeks, so I thought to myself, "Yey! I would at least have another person to talk to, instead of just Diego, the dog!"

Gearárd, My Human Walking Partner

Gearárd was quite good-looking, very strong and gentle, yet there was something scary in him that I couldn't really put my finger on. We became good friends in a very short time. To keep him from getting bored, he invited me once to explore the mountain with him. He didn't have to ask me a second time.

So now it was Gearárd, Diego, and I who would walk up and down Montagne d'amour. I enjoyed having Gearárd lead me and show me places. He would courageously venture into areas where there was no trail, assuring me that it was okay. He'd go first, and then if things were clear he'd come back to tell me to come follow him, and I would. In the difficult parts of the trail, he would hold my hand to help me up.

He was very strong, and at one time he pulled me up from a deep ravine. I saw Diego looking at me, seemingly relieved that he didn't have to pull me up this time. Gearárd and I had some very good talks, and he quickly became my walking partner for about three weeks.

Gearard seemed to have many things I wanted in a man. He was handsome and had a mind and a will of his own. He was very funny and made me laugh a lot. I enjoyed having to depend on him on our mountain hikes. He had a sensitive soul. He asked me good questions to draw me out and listened well to my words, even to the things I didn't say. It was good to be around a man like him who simply enjoyed me, and my womanliness.

Then one afternoon, Gearárd came to my house and said he had to leave the mountain in two days since he had finally found an apartment he liked. I was quite disappointed that he had to leave so soon. He asked if he could cook dinner for me the next evening as his going-away celebration with me. The following day, we walked together for the last time, and at night he made me a wonderful dinner of Irish stew, pork chops, and salad. We said our goodbyes, and I said that I would miss him. He said he would miss me, too. He walked me back to my house, and we had a final cup of coffee. I offered to pray for him, and soon he had to go back to his loft.

As he stepped out of my cabin, I had tears in my eyes. I didn't understand then what was going on. Because I was alone, I let myself cry for hours, heaving as I cried. I couldn't understand my emotions. I cried out to God, asking, "Lord, why? Why is there such a man and I know he's not mine? Why can't a man like him be mine?"

In tears, I rocked myself to sleep like a baby.

All I Wanted To Do Was To Cry

As I look back on that episode now, I can honestly say that I did not have any romantic emotions for Gearárd. I did not have a crush on him nor was I in love with him. I did not envision him to be a boyfriend or husband. I don't even think I wanted him to stay for me either. At that time, all I wanted to do was cry....or grieve is a better term.

I grieved that I could only have a taste of what I wanted but may never have. Maybe it was too painful to accept that my heart was ready to love; yet there was no man to give my heart to.

"Why is there a man and he's not mine, God?"

Gearárd represented some of the things I wanted in a man, at least when it came to his physical features and capabilities. He represented courage in venturing into dangerous unknown trails; leadership in guiding me as I followed him; strength in pulling me out of a pit; and gentleness in preparing me Irish stew.

Those traits are probably some of the things many women want in a man. Don't we just want to have our hearts and souls rest in someone we can trust to lead us? Don't we want to be relieved of the pressure of having to be strong or in control all the time, simply because a good man is leading? Don't we all just want to be able to trust a man and rest in the goodness of his heart?

This experience is just one of the many pictures in my journey with men. In my younger years there were quite a few significant men who shaped my idea of a man and in the process also shaped my view of God in significant ways.

My hope is to lead us to a place where we can think through our singleness and come out of this experience learning to entrust our souls to the real Love of our hearts, the same One who rocked me in His arms as I cried. I want you to live well as a single woman who knows where her heart is anchored, who knows where to go when she feels the pangs of loneliness, and how to help others even as she struggles in her own soul.

I want that for me. I want that for you.

Journaling my Thoughts

★ What is it that you want in a man?

★ What is it that you want in a relationship?

★ Write an honest letter to God in the space below, sharing with Him your deepest heart's desires.

The Delight in His Eyes

CHAPTER TWO

2 The Delight In His Eyes

Orpah Omega Lee. I like my name. I also like how my father named us, his children, after characters of the Bible. Orpah is from the book of Ruth in the Old Testament. I was named Omega because my parents knew I would be the last fruit of my mother's pregnancy. Lee came from the first letters of my father and mother's names: Leonardo and Elayda.

I know a little bit about being delighted in by a man because of my father, Rev. Leonardo D. Marasigan. My *Tatay*[1] is a retired pastor of a small Presbyterian church in the Philippines. Yes, I am a genuine, pure-blooded PK, or Preacher's kid.

Tatay was designed by God to be a lively, sanguine individual. If he saw you today, he would greet you with his wide 88-year-old smile, saying, "God loves you and I love you!" If you were a visitor in my church, you would either be taken aback by this funny, crazy-looking old man or feel truly welcomed and loved in the church. *Tatay* loves talking to people and making them feel at home. Above all, he likes talking about Jesus to just about anyone he meets.

My father was the first representation to me of a big and good God. When I was small, he had the habit of taking my hand and comparing it against his huge hand and then thumping my hand against his big tummy so that it made a loud hollow sound. He would then take my feet and compare them against his huge feet. I always thought he was

[1] *Tatay*, pronounced /t´ɑːtɑːy/, is the Filipino word for "father."

a big and powerful man. At night I would pretend to be asleep on the sofa just so that he would carry me to my bed. As a kid, my favorite game with *Tatay* was "horsey-horsey." He would sit on his chair, stick out his feet, and let me step on those feet. Then he would swing his legs up and down while I screamed in delight.

Tatay is a good person. He has many faults, yes, but I believe that when he looks and deals with me as his daughter, he wants only what is good for me. He had rules in the house and if you didn't do what he said, he could get very scary because of his loud voice. Young as I was, I understood that those rules were for my good and if I disobeyed, there would be painful consequences.

Tatay and God Were Good Friends

Tatay helped usher me to an understanding of God because of the way I saw him relate to God. I would see him read his Bible everyday and he encouraged us when we were little to do the same. I saw him pray to God in a very personal and honoring way. He showed me that he and God were good friends.

Tatay proved to me that when he prayed, God would always answer. Being the baby in the family, I would always get attention whenever I got a headache or tummy ache. But whatever sickness it was, I would always wait for him to pray for me so that he could ask God to heal me. When he prayed, my aches would instantly go away.

I remember many times when my *Tatay* would look at me with much delight in his eyes, while he exclaimed, "My beautiful daughter!" I grew up believing I was beautiful because he said so. He was a demonstrative man who was never afraid to kiss my cheeks or embrace me in public. Even now that I am a grown woman, this 88-year-old man never fails to affirm me with his words and touch.

He Who Touches You, Touches The Apple Of His Eye

Today I only get to visit him on Sundays but I still see those delight-filled eyes of his. I can better understand the verse in Zechariah 2:8b

"...for he who touches you, touches the apple of His eye" mainly because of what I saw in my father's eyes when he looked at me.

It is always fun watching *Tatay* laugh and celebrate anything with a dance! Even now in his old age, when he is happy about something, he gives us his wide smile and then slowly wriggles and sways his hips and hands. That is "*Tatay's* happy dance." Much later, I would discover this character of God in His word in Zephaniah 3:17: "The Lord your God is in your midst, a victorious warrior. He will exult over you with joy, He will be quiet in His love, He will rejoice over you with shouts of joy." Another verse that speaks of God's extravagant love is in Jeremiah 31:3: "The Lord appeared to us in the past, saying: I have loved you with an everlasting love; I have drawn you with unfailing kindness."

Because *Tatay* showed me how he rejoiced over me, it became easy for me to understand that there is a God who loves me, a God of fun and laughter, who welcomes me with delight and wants me to be with Him forever. I think that is why, until now, words of affirmation and loving touches are what mostly convey love to me. I know that today, when my father sees me, his eyes will sparkle as if he just saw a beautiful princess, and drawing his breath, he will take me into his arms and kiss me, saying "My beautiful Orpah!"

Jesus Christ, The Anchor Of My Soul

When I was a child, my parents introduced me to God and His Son Jesus Christ. I was taught to memorize the King James Version Bible of John 3:16, which says, "For God so loved the world, that He gave His only begotten Son, that whoever believes in Him shall not perish, but have eternal life." They taught us a song, "Jesus loves me this I know, for the Bible tells me so. Little ones to Him belong, they are weak but He is strong! Yes, Jesus loves me, the Bible tells me so."

I began to understand how all of these things about God related to me personally when my eldest sister brought me along with her to attend a meeting called College Life at her university in 1973. I listened to a man named Dr. Bill Bright, founder of Campus Crusade for Christ International. That year, he came to the Philippines to speak to a group of college kids about having a personal relationship with God through His Son, Jesus Christ. That same night, Dr. Bill Bright invited us to give our hearts to Jesus Christ. As a 12-year-old, I gave my life to Jesus and asked Him to be my personal Savior and Lord through a simple prayer of faith. I repeated the prayer that Dr. Bill Bright said and made it my own. It said something like this:

> *Lord Jesus Christ, I need you. I am not sure I have welcomed you into my heart yet, but today, I open the door of my life and receive you as my personal Savior and Lord. Come into my heart. Come and change my heart. Thank you for the forgiveness of my sins. Thank you for the hope of eternal life. Come and make me the kind of person you want me to be. Amen!*

Since that time, and throughout my whole life, Jesus Christ has been the anchor of my soul. He gives me deep joy and rest as I face all the uncertainties, difficulties and turmoil of the world around me.

I discovered that I could talk to Him through simple prayers and He would talk to me through His written word, the Bible, which became His love letters to me. As I walked with Him more, I learned to enjoy Him and embrace Him as my source of love and true significance.

I basked in the promises that He gave me. The following passage from Psalm 139:13 NASB became precious to me:

> For You formed my inward parts; You wove me in my mother's womb. I will give thanks to You, for I am fearfully and wonderfully made; Wonderful are Your works, and my soul knows it very well.

My picture of God gradually changed from being just the Creator and Savior who saved me and died for me through His Son Jesus Christ, to becoming the personal God who loved everything about me and knew me inside out including my future. Now, I know Him even deeper as the True Lover of my Soul.

One of my favorite singers, Tramaine Hawkins, once sang a beautiful song that puts into words and music what I feel about my Sweet Jesus. This is the anthem of my soul:

> You Are My Life[2]
> I needed someone, Someone to hold my hand
> To get me through and understand.
> You are my life! You are my destiny!
> You are my days, my nights,
> You mean the world to me!
> You are the Star that lights my way,
> Guides me through my darkest days.
> You're my life! You are my love!
> You give me joy, joy that I have never known.
> With You here by my side,
> I'll never be alone. You're my Heaven in all of its glory,
> You're my True Love Story.
> You're my Life, You are my Love!
> When I'm feeling low, I know you'll make me smile again.
> When there's no place to turn I know that you'll be there.
> And if ever I needed someone, Someone to hold my hand.
> I know you'll get me through, I know you'll understand.
> You are my life, You are my destiny.
> You are my days, my nights, you mean the world to me.
> You're my heaven in all of its glory,
> You're my true love Story.
> You're my life, Lord, You are my love!

This song expresses in words and melody exactly what I would like to say to God, if I were facing Him today. It is only fitting that my heart should respond in this way because God initiated this love relationship with me first.

I thank God for the good relationship I had with my earthly father, who delighted in me and helped paint a wonderful picture of my Heavenly Father. That relationship now has allowed me to experience Jesus Christ as the One True Lover of my soul.

---

[2] Tramaine Hawkins, "You Are My Life," *The Joy That Floods My Soul* (Sparrow/Capitol, 1988 cd).

Journaling my Thoughts

★ What is your father like? How would you describe your relationship with him?

★ In what ways has this view of your earthly father affected your current view of your Heavenly Father?

★Who is Jesus Christ to you and what is your relationship with Him?

★How do you think God delights in you?

★Would you like to know God personally? Appendix B speaks of a God who desires to have an intimate personal relationship with us. Reading this section, what is your response to His offer of love and forgiveness?

★Write your letter and prayer to God here.

I was 17...

OOOPS...
He's Married.

CHAPTER THREE

3 OOPS, He's Married!

My first boyfriend was a married man. There. I said it. Yes, he was someone else's husband. Not mine.

I attended many seminars on "Love Courtship and Marriage" when I was 13 and a new believer in Jesus Christ. One of the things that the speakers emphasized was that Christian single women should pray that God would give them good, godly, single men who would love God first and their wives second. Then in marriage, they would love each other and spend their lives serving God together as a couple.

This idealistic picture of a man-woman relationship almost sounded like a curse for me because through the years, I felt I didn't belong to that category of single women who were blessed to have such a man. Unfortunately, I made personal choices along the way that defied all that was taught at these talks and led me into messy predicaments.

Longings Awake

At 17, I was introduced to the world of men and my heart was awakened by longings that I was not familiar with. Being raised in a Christian family, we were not exposed to the reality of temptations and the subtleties of worldly attractions. These were things we simply didn't talk about. I was naïve about life and love.

My parents normally would not allow any of my siblings to get out and play with the neighborhood kids. But knowing that I was the very active child who loved sports and thought nothing of climbing trees and getting dirty on the streets, they allowed me to play volleyball in our neighborhood. My mother probably thought I needed less protection from the outside world and that I was brave enough to be out there and take care of myself.

In our neighborhood lived Anton. He was 25, and worked as a marketing person of a food company. Since he lived nearby, he would come to all our neighborhood games to cheer us on. Sometimes he assisted our volleyball coach during inter-neighborhood competitions. He was friendly with all the girls and I thought he was such a nice and fun person. Once, my teammates invited me to a birthday party where this man engaged me in an interesting conversation. There, I met his wife and their small daughter and I thought, "Wow, what a nice, small family..."

I was surprised when later, in the same party, Anton took me aside and told me that he wanted to visit me at school. I didn't know how to respond to that and wondered why he wanted to do that. I think my silence meant yes to him.

Off I Went... To See And Find Out

I was flattered by what I heard, but something in my system told me something was definitely wrong with this picture. My mind protested, "Stop, stop, he's married!" But another part of me said, "Hmmm... this feels so good, I wonder what he's up to... and besides, we're just being friendly, he's such a nice guy, how can I turn him down?" So you see, there was a debate going on inside me—and the impulse that told me it was all right since it felt good, won in the electoral process in my brain. So off I went... to see and find out.

Ever since that party, I would see him almost every morning waiting for me at the bus stop corner to make sure he rode with me to my school and see me off to my class. Sometimes on my way home from classes, I would see him waiting for me outside the school gate. He would ask me out to dinner or movies, and I would say yes.

At first I always asked what he thought his wife would say if she knew, and he would reply, "I really don't love my wife. I was just forced into marriage with her because she got pregnant with my daughter. If I had a choice, I would take my daughter and go away with you." He would also tell me, "My Mom and my siblings don't like my wife. My Mom hates her guts and my siblings always don't seem to like her at all. I like you, Orpah, and I told them about you and they like you a lot, too."

The Hiding Begins

As much as possible Anton would prevent me from talking about his wife and family. Conversations should always be about enjoying the present, about us.

Anton spent hours discovering things that I liked and things that would give me joy. His desire was to please me in every way he could. He would ask me what I enjoyed the most—the flowers I liked, the songs I listened to, and the food I wanted to eat.

Anton always had nice words to say about how I looked. He affirmed good things about me. I melted at his words, and he won my heart more and more.

His visits became more frequent, and this time it was I who expected him to come and bring me to school, fetch me in the afternoons and hang out with me for hours.

I looked forward to our movie dates where we could be freer to express our affection by holding hands, hugging and kissing. When we were together, we would talk and talk and wait until it was time for him to go home to his wife. My love language being quality time, my hunger for love was filled as we watched movies, or just did nothing together on rainy days. All that time, my brain and my heart battled inside me: Was I not a pastor's kid? Should I be holding this married man's hand or kissing him? But this was just an innocent friendship!"

I went out with this man for about eight months. Yes, it took that long for me to actually figure out my relationship with Anton because I enjoyed having a man in my life. He pursued my heart, and enjoyed my femininity. He made me feel that I needed his advice. He even sang to me. That was what I loved the most about him. He lavished attention on me and expressed his desire for me. I was the one who always held back. So why couldn't I enjoy this guy and keep him for a while? After all, we were not sleeping together.

On three separate occasions Anton tried to entice me to get away with him for a whole day outside the city. He would say "Orpah, let's drive up to Baguio and stay there till dinner, then we'll return by dinner or right before midnight. No one will even know we're gone. Let's just tell them you need to be with Liza (my friend) for the evening." Then he would tell me the places he wanted me to see, especially the folk houses where he used to sing.

In all those three occasions, he never forced me. The more accurate words would be that he flirtatiously enticed me to go away with him. I was so tempted to throw caution to the wind and say yes. If I did, who knows what would have happened to us? Each time he invited me, something in me just didn't feel good about going out with him. I felt fear. Fear about what my father would say. Fear about myself, because I probably knew that if I had gone with him, there would have been no way I could have turned back. Today I know it was God protecting me, sparing me the possibility of an unwanted pregnancy or a more messed up life.

But in my naiveté, I convinced myself that I was doing all right as long as I was not sleeping with Anton and not hurting anyone else.

Lying and Hiding is Part of the Deal

One part of me realized that no matter how much Anton tried to convince me that he had been forced into a shotgun wedding and that he never liked his wife, he still could not be fully mine. I knew his heart belonged to his wife and could not be shared with me. But another part of me kept pretending we were not doing anything wrong. I was torn between my heart and my mind.

We were always hiding in case anyone from his family and friends would see us together. I had to live a lie too because even when I was seeing this man, I still attended Bible Studies in school, went to church, sang in choir and acted like nothing wrong was happening.

After a date with me, he would go home to his wife and lie to her about where he came from. In the months that followed, no one knew about our relationship except my best friend in the volleyball team, and my sister, Ammi.

The first time I told Ammi that I was going out with Anton, she listened patiently, trying to understand me. I knew she felt she had to keep her anger to herself, because otherwise I would never speak to her about it again. Instead, she lovingly encouraged me to get out of the relationship fast, while I still could. I promised her I would. I told her that I didn't like it anymore anyway and was going to end it soon. But I continued seeing Anton. To keep my relationship with her, I had to lie to her. I made her believe that I had broken off with Anton but in reality I was still so much in a relationship with him. Later, Ammi found out about all my lies. I also came to know to my great shame that the whole neighborhood, except his wife, had already known about my illicit relationship with Anton.

I did not see the whole gamut of lies and deceptions Anton was spinning before his family and before me. Neither did I see what a liar I was becoming to my family and to my God. I lived with the struggle that though I liked, or maybe loved, this man, it was not right. I felt this nagging guilt that Someone was looking and saw everything that was going on. Deep down I knew it was wrong.

It wasn't long before something had to give.

Journaling my Thoughts

★ Is this chapter relevant to you or to a friend?

★ Are you currently in a relationship with a married man?

★ What keeps you in this relationship?

★ The longer you stay in this relationship, what do you think is at stake?

★ Write your letter to God here.

Lord, I'm tired. I want out!

CHAPTER FOUR

N.Y.C. TAXI

4 Lord I'm tired. I want out!

Women, single and married, have come to me and asked, "Orpah, I love this man but he's married. That's okay, isn't it? I don't think this is adultery, because we're not sleeping together. Besides, he still goes home to his wife and he merely shares with me deep things about himself..."

I have made many small decisions in the past that led to bigger decisions that later became huge, terrible actions. My initial point of decision came when Anton asked to pick me up from my school. Right then, I could have said "No" and walked away, but part of me also wanted to know what would happen if I stayed.

I realize that I probably went ahead with this relationship with Anton because I did not have enough fear of God. I did not know full well the gravity of the pain it would cause the people around me including the family of this man. Most of all I did not fully understand that it was sin in God's eyes. So, like a naughty, deceitful child, I dipped my hand into the cookie jar, and grieved my God.

All throughout the eight months, I enjoyed my relationship with Anton. I enjoyed having a man think of me, spend time with me, and dote on me. Maybe I also had that sick sense of wondering how it would all end. Anton was very good to me, so I really had no reason to break up this relationship. I was enjoying it so much! As long as I was able to stand the hiding and the double life I was leading, I was good to go.

I Was Never Part Of The Picture

Seven months into the relationship, Anton started becoming less available. There were times when I wanted to meet up with him, but his wife wanted him to go with her somewhere, so he had to turn me down. One night he had to cut short our date because he said he had an activity to do with his wife. Our routine was, I would go ahead of him in a cab and he would come home after ten minutes in another cab. That particular night, he went on ahead of me and asked me to wait a few minutes before I came home. While in the cab I saw them walking up the road holding hands, looking as though I was never part of the picture. And the truth was, really, I was not, could never be, part of the picture.

More incidents like this happened where I became second priority. Initially I found all his apologies acceptable, but when it happened more often than I wanted, I began to tire of this set up. I wanted more. The truth was, Anton could not give me more than what he was already giving, so it left me more and more disappointed. It came to a point where I thought to myself, "This is crazy. I believe I am worth much more than this." After a few months of hiding and lying and being second priority in his life, I sincerely prayed in my heart, "Lord, I'm tired. I want out!"

I probably said that line about 20 times on different occasions in the span of eight months. I would resolve in my heart that I was going to end this relationship that very day! But it was always a battle. Why should I stop it? It just showed me how weak my flesh was because I thought that there was no reason for me to break up with the man. He was a good man, he loved me, he was not taking advantage of me—or so I thought. He spent time with me and wanted to be with me. Everything else was right—except that he was married and he was not all mine.

God Sets Up An End To The Affair

I believe that when a woman comes to the point when she really wants out of an affair and silently asks God, "Help, I can't do it, You've got to help me get out of this!" God answers that prayer. God sets up an end to the affair even if it has to take humiliating encounters.

In my story, God had to step in and heed my cry for help but not without letting me experience hurtful and shameful events.

God in His sovereignty helped me get out of my relationship with Anton by exposing all the lies he made toward his wife, and all the lies I made. To make a long story short, we were found out

The Real Story Unfolds

To save his neck, Anton told his wife that even if I'd known he was married, I asked him to come to my school. He said that I was the one who persistently called him to meet with him and because I was persistent, he could not turn me down. He said that I was the one who was trying to keep a relationship with him all this time. That was all I needed to hear for me to be angry enough to really want to get out of the relationship.

The affair ended like so much of the mess we see in soap operas where the wife confronts the other woman. But in my case, the wife did not confront me. She went straight to my father, the pastor, the man who delighted in me! She appealed to my father to make me stop my affair with her husband.

I think what truly broke my heart was when I saw my father cry in hurt and in agony. My father didn't know what to do; he probably wanted to kill me. But in hurt and shame, he just wept. That did it for me. I said in my heart, "Enough!"

The Hurt Father Heart

I had to ask forgiveness from my parents and each of my siblings. This was probably one of the most difficult times in my life. Yet this story has allowed me to understand better what grace and the love of family meant. I understood a lot more about the gravity of sin and how it hurts the Father heart of God because of the way it hurt my earthly father.

In a shame-based culture like mine, the consequences of that experience were not only deep shame in the community—because a pastor's kid became a mistress—but also the hindrance to the work of

God in that place. I think that we were never able to share the gospel of Jesus Christ in that community again. My family used to be very active in sharing the gospel, distributing relief goods, and sharing about Jesus with our neighbors during calamities. All of a sudden, all of these stopped and we became quiet. Neighbors gossiped and I walked in shame everyday when I went to school.

God in His goodness has taken my story and redeemed it to be used in my life and in the lives of many individuals. As a counselor, I meet many men and women who come to me and tell me their stories. I tell them, "Get out NOW. I know what I am saying. I've been there, I've done it and I tell you it's not worth it, get out!" They can't tell me, "How do you know, you don't understand" because they know I've been through it. When I say this to them, they know that it is with utmost love, compassion and understanding. I won't stop until they have heard me well. I make it a point to enter into their story and expose the lie they've come to believe, even if it means risking my relationship with them.

Usually my friends will hate me for a while. But I don't care if they do. If I love my friends enough, I'll be willing to take their hate and angry words knowing that afterwards they'll appreciate what I've done. If not, that's okay. This is kingdom work. I see this as part of the job God has given me and I intend to do it faithfully.

My counseling mentor always tells me, "We cannot be passive observers. If you are not doing anything to right a wrong, you are part of the problem. And God will make us accountable."[3]

The Hard Climb Back

It was only by God's grace that I came out of that experience in one piece. I had one bout of depression and some instances of wanting to kill myself during the worst times of that mess because I had a hard time dealing with the guilt and shame that I had brought into this wonderful pastor's family. I contemplated going to a beach and walking into the

[3] Dr. Philip G. Ney would often stress this point in his lectures on Counseling and in my conversations with him at Mt. Joy College, Victoria, British Columbia, February 1999.

water until I drowned. Satan's accusing words often rang out loud and strong in my ears, "How could you do such a thing!? You, a pastor's kid!? What shame have you given your whole family! You really are the black sheep of this family, aren't you? You bring them shame!"

It took me about two years to finally feel and know I was okay again. It took a lot of feeding my mind and heart with the truth of God's grace and forgiveness that I needed to receive and claim for myself. It involved a lot of going to God's Word and being around loving Christian friends who were willing to walk with me through that difficult time.

However, my father's trust was one thing I had to earn back. Before this painful event, my father allowed himself to be involved in the affairs of my heart. He would ask me who my crushes were and he would either say, "He's ugly," or "He's ok," indicating his interest in that part of my life. After this event, I never heard him ask anything about this area of my heart. I felt he did not care or even want to care. Silence was all there was between us. Maybe this was his way of dealing with his hurt. His silence grieved me much more than he could have imagined. There were other guys who wanted to take me out but I would always feel I did not deserve to have a boyfriend again.

Picking Up The Broken Pieces & Giving Them To God

I believe it took *Tatay* 20 years before he involved himself again in the affairs of my heart. I was driving one day with him and my *Nanay*[4]. I was just coming out of a painful, disappointing relationship with a younger man and I nonchalantly said, "*Tatay*, I'm broken hearted! You remember this guy who comes to our house? Well it didn't work out and I'm very sad." Then there was silence, and I suddenly remembered, "Oh, I forgot, we don't talk about this stuff." But then he broke his silence and said, "Well, you just have to pick up the broken pieces and give them to God." That was all he said. It gave me both relief as well as pain to realize that I missed hearing my father speak to my heart like that.

[4] *Nanay*, pronounced /n´ɑːnɑːy/, is the Filipino word for "mother."

Now as I'm writing this, I'm wondering how all these things have affected the way I relate with men. Maybe I feel I don't deserve a good man. Maybe I feel no single man would ever like me.

Why is there a man and he's not mine? The speakers who spoke on "Love, Courtship and Marriage" when I was 13 were right. It is still worth praying for a godly, single man whose heart will become mine alone. Today, I live my life with no illusion that I am invulnerable to sin. This makes me more dependent on God the Holy Spirit to live my life in and through me. I am grateful that God can use a life like mine to help redeem other people's lives so that they start living out God's story.

God in His amazing grace has truly saved a wretch like me and has spared me the agony of being with a man who can never be mine, and possibly even spared me the difficulties of being a single mom. God in His abounding grace was able to show me clearly that He has forgiven all my sins, including this sin, by dying on the cross for me. I thank God for His grace and love and the joy of reconciliation.

Please read Appendix A:
"The Dynamics of Adultery in the Christian Community."
How does one fall into adultery and what should one do to get out of it?

Journaling my Thoughts

★If you are in a relationship with a married man, what would it take for you to get out of it?

★Has this chapter prompted you to do something about this relationship? In what way?

★Do you have any friend who is currently involved with a married man? How would you like to help her?

★Write your letter and prayer to God here.

To All
the Men
I've Loved
Before
CHAPTER FIVE

5 To All the Men I've Loved Before

Paul was the man I almost married. Only he never asked... He gave me a small picture of him and at the back he wrote me a poem:

> I am going through life
> seeking wonderful hours
> but the ones I spent with you
> will I cherish most....

Sounds sweet, huh? For three years, three months, and three days, that poem became my anchor in my hope for a serious relationship with him. I waited for him, but this man who said he loved me never asked me to marry him and never became mine. It almost sounds like another telenovela, doesn't it?

Someone once asked me, "Orpah, if all the men you've loved before were all widowed and single again and have become millionaires, whom would you choose?"

I said, "Hands down, I would choose Paul! On the premise that he has gone through Hope Alive counseling therapy, he has become a widower, and I am still strong enough to walk down the aisle!"

The Baby-Faced Heartthrob

I met Paul when I was in college. He was the cute baby-faced heartthrob of our school. Oddly enough, when I first saw him I couldn't figure out why the girls would swoon over him because I felt he was just a boy.

My friend Marianne and I dared each other to ask Paul out to dinner just to find out what he was made of and what he was like. Our dinner ended well, we got to know him a little bit, and the three of us made a pact to pray for each other. What developed was a great friendship among the three of us. When my dear friend Marianne got married, Paul and I were left to ourselves. Somewhere along the way, he showed he liked me, and later I knew I liked him, too.

Paul and I continued to have dinners and lunches together. He took me to observe his ministries, brought me to his friends' church, and introduced me to his family. On one particular birthday, I was the only guest he invited to his home. I enjoyed talking, laughing and sharing my heart with Paul. On Valentine's Day, he sent me a small card with a poem that read:

Ever-dearest Orpah,
My heart rejoices in the Lord
For such a chord as you
'Tis like sweet music in the air
The love I share with you
It's so beautiful to be true... You're my Valentine!

One time, he suddenly announced that he had to leave the city to go up to Baguio, north of the Philippines, for graduate studies. During that time, there were no emails or cell phones, just telegrams and snail mail. The day before he left, although he was living only a few streets next to mine, he sent me a telegram saying in Tagalog, "Goodbye, I leave tomorrow."

Two weeks after he left, he wrote me a letter asking if I had "received a piece of paper with words I wrote having you in mind?" He had written me a poem that went this way:

I Thought You Were Here
A glance through the window, a breeze of fresh air,
And for a brief moment I thought you were there.
The sound of sweet music, the joy in my heart
Would turn to deep sorrow, to know we're apart
What curse is this for me that time dare not heal?
Too long it would linger, the sadness I feel

A glance through the window, a breeze of fresh air,
And for a brief moment I thought you were there.

If you were in my place and received poems like these, what would you have thought and felt?

Paul managed to convince a friend to bring beautiful roses down from Baguio to my home. I love flowers. I love roses and tulips. Anytime a man gives me flowers, my heart leaps. I came home and saw beautiful red roses all over my house. I was thrilled to death!

My Picture on His Wall

That summer, I had a chance to climb a small mountain, Sto. Tomas, in Baguio with a group of friends. I thought it would be a great idea to visit Paul. When I came to his campus, I was amused to find that everyone there, especially the women, knew who I was and that I was coming that weekend. When Paul's best friend Gerry and I entered Paul's dorm room, imagine my surprise when the very first thing we saw as we entered was my picture! It was hanging on the wall right across the door. No wonder some of his girl friends on campus were looking strangely at me. I figured they recognized me from the picture in his room. Another surprising thing was that Gerry, his best friend and roommate practically knew everything about me. All these flattered me, but something in my gut told me that something was not quite right about all these.

I think I was smart enough to sense that Paul must have led people, especially the women in his campus, to believe that we had a more serious relationship than we really had, and that this might have been to his advantage. I found out from Gerry that so many women were swooning over him. My brain quickly thought that he probably used me to ward off the women who were falling in love with him. It was his way of saying to them all: "Back off, I'm taken!" It must have worked. Up to this day I can't exactly tell what he said to them but I'm quite sure, as I was back then, that none of the girls around the campus were happy at seeing my picture in Paul's room and none of them were happy I came at all. I didn't get a chance to confirm this but it hung over my head as I came out of his campus that day.

Paul and I maintained our relationship through letters. He would write me to say hello and update me about his studies. Each time Valentine's Day came around, he would send me letters and poems. He made me feel special. Paul didn't say he loved me, but all the time he behaved as though he wanted to court me, making me believe that it was just a matter of time before he did. And so I waited.

The Death of a Dream

Over time, there were less letters, and less of him. Eventually he came back to the city and one summer night, he called to ask if we could meet and talk, because that same month, he said, he was about to marry someone else.

When I heard that, my heart died.

On the night we met, I intended to make Paul know everything about how I felt about our relationship. I was living in an apartment then with some other girlfriends and I remember I was so nervous and scared to meet him that night. My knees and my hands were shaking and my friend Janine had to embrace me and assure me that everything was going to be all right. She encouraged me to be brave and tell him everything I wanted to tell him. All of my housemates were praying and they stayed upstairs while I met Paul in our dining room.

I vaguely remember how he started the conversation but I remember feeling so anxious because I knew I would be exposing myself to him. It was frightening to be vulnerable. When I got the chance to talk, I told him that one of my greatest hurts was that though he lavishly showed me he loved me, he never said the words. Instead he led me to believe and hope that there was more to our friendship.

Then he cut me short and said, "You know, Orpah, there was a time I told my parents that if I were to marry anyone, it would be you, Orpah…"

I was surprised. "Why didn't you tell me?" I asked. He told me that he got scared. In my brain I asked, "Scared of what? Why didn't you speak up?"

He said that when he went out with me he felt like I did not need him. He thought I was doing very well in my life and my ministry. I looked content with my life and did not seem to need a man, not even him.

I thought, "Had you asked me, I would have dropped everything and followed you!" Why didn't he? I never asked and I will never know.

After that two-hour talk, Paul and I prayed and cried together and he, for the first time, spoke the words I'd always wanted to hear: "I love you." My response was "Thank you!" His admission validated what I knew all along. Somehow I couldn't tell him I loved him too because he was walking someone else down the aisle the following month. Our story ended with a small kiss, a tight embrace, and a good goodbye.

As I was trying to understand what happened between Paul and myself, my hypothesis then was that maybe, Paul really did love me and maybe he really did want to marry me. I would like to believe that he was telling the truth. But I needed to know in my heart why he did not choose to marry me.

Looking back, I remember the times that Paul would ask me what I thought about missions. We were still dating then. Paul's heart was to be a missionary to some remote area in Southeast Asia. He had so much passion about missions that we would discuss books about Jim Elliot and many other missionaries' stories that he'd read. He wanted to go where no other missionaries had gone.

I, on the other hand, had no idea then about "missions" or any passion for it. I had just given up my veterinary practice to work full time with Campus Crusade as a missionary to TV and movie personalities. I did not understand or share Paul's passion for missions in the sense of going off to some hinterland to share the gospel there. We were called to opposite directions. I felt called to minister to the rich and famous; he wanted to be a missionary to the poor.

Paul was probably right when he said he felt I did not need him. Part of my damaged heart, I would discover later, was that I had made a commitment to not make people think that I was weak and that I needed them. I did not want to make people see my vulnerability and tenderness. Paul probably never saw those parts of me that were soft, welcoming and delightful. All he saw was a woman who had her life all put together and it was probably difficult for him to see where he would fit in my life and where he would feel needed.

Looking back, I should have asked him, "So why are you doing all these, Paul?" But in those days, a girl was never to ask a man. We were supposed to wait! Now, of course I think that's all nonsense. Paul and I had a relationship that lasted more than three years. After all those years, should I have asked? Absolutely! But I was young and naïve.

An Unspoken Agreement

It's been 20 years now since that painful night. Paul and I had an unspoken agreement to not be involved in each other's lives. To honor his married life, I did not want to know too much about him and he never made any effort to continue our friendship or communicate. However, well-meaning friends, and especially Gerry, would update both of us once in a while about each other.

Do I think of Paul at all or regret that he was never mine? Yes, there were times when I wondered what my life would have been like if I were Mrs. Paul. But I needed to say goodbye to all that and sever all my ties with him so that his wife would have a chance to become a happy wife, and my husband-to-be (whoever he is) would have all the chance to be a happy husband.

This year, Paul came home alone from abroad. Gerry arranged for Paul and myself to have dinner with him and his wife. This was going to be the first time I'd be seeing Paul again after all these years.

It was so good to see Paul still looking handsome and charming as ever, but somehow the joy and the glitter in his eyes had faded. I felt very sad to hear from him that his marriage was an unhappy one. He has a son whom he loves more than anything in the world but his wife had been trying to divorce him for the past five years. He never became a missionary to Southeast Asia. For some reason, all his dreams were put aside. Meanwhile he worked as a salesman for a car company but hoped to get a more lucrative job in the future. I grieved to see how his soul had died. I wanted so much to help him in any way, but I knew I couldn't and I shouldn't.

We had a great dinner date together. As we parted that night with a warm embrace, I offered a prayer for Paul that God in His goodness would somehow restore his marriage and Paul could find deep joy again.

I couldn't help wondering, did Paul make a mistake in marrying his wife instead of me? And if so, was I still single because Paul made that mistake? Did we both miss out on God's will? Will I ever know the answers to these questions? Maybe, not until I get to heaven. All I know is that I loved Paul once in my lifetime. I will always continue to want the best for this man, and pray that he will find love and meaning in his life again.

Today I'm very glad I didn't marry Paul because, if I did...well, you wouldn't be reading this book!

Journaling my Thoughts

★ If you were to marry now and all the men you've loved before were all widowed and single again and have become successful in life, whom would you choose? Why?

★ Why do you think your past relationships didn't work?

★ What was your role in the breakup of your relationship?

★ Were you able to have a proper goodbye with a man you've loved before? If not, what can you do to sever all ties from this man? e.g. return all his gifts, have a symbolic cremation of all his letters, donate all his jewelry to an orphanage, move out of the house he gave you, etc...

★ If you were given a chance to retrace your steps, what would you have done right?

★ Would you like to go to God now and tell Him the things you've grieved about but never had the chance or courage to voice out? Write your letter and your prayer to God here.

Waiting is an Awful Word

CHAPTER SIX

6 Waiting is an Awful Word

The word "awful" has two meanings. In one sense it means "very bad or unpleasant." In another, older sense it means being filled with "reverential respect mixed with fear or wonder." Childbirth is "awful" in both senses of the word.

Veterinary Obstetrics was my favorite subject in college because I came face to face with a life born in front of me. Even the dirtiest, smelly goat gives birth to beautiful, soft-coated kids! I have helped two human beings, dogs, a cat, a goat, a cow, and a horse give birth. I can say that giving birth is always a matter of life and death for any species. The pain of labor is something I'm glad I'll never experience, but my work as a veterinarian has made me witness it time and again. I have heard all the groans and seen the huge interplay of all the muscles that contract and pelvises that expand in the process. While the pain is unimaginable for single women like us, all human mothers will attest that they felt like they would almost die!

The amazing thing though is that as soon as the mother gives birth, the pain she experiences fades away and is quickly forgotten. Having waited patiently for nine months, the mother finds herself quickly reverting from an awful, pain-filled situation into relief as she welcomes, with awful wonder, this little person in her arms.

The hope of seeing her baby come out will make any mother willing to undergo extreme pain, and meet it with courage and joy. The experience becomes even more meaningful when she has her husband with her to help her through the pain and share the joy with her. Soon enough, overwhelming relief and happiness quickly replace the pain of childbirth when a newborn comes out at the appointed time. It is a beautiful, miraculous experience designed by our Creator.

The same is true for a woman who waits and trusts in God. Such a woman trusts that in the midst of the pain of disappointment or loss, something beautiful will come out. She will courageously go on through life however painful it will be, trusting that though she may not get all the things she wants now, yet God will do something awesome and wonderful and beautiful in her life.

Waiting Exposed

Looking back at my story with Paul, I felt that God had set me up to wait on Him. Waiting on the Lord developed my character. It led me to the feet of Him who knew my heart. Waiting on God also exposed my true heart. It exposed the small god of the self that I worshiped in contrast to the real God who was sovereign over my heart and life.

A speaker in our Southeast Asia leadership conference once said that when we cannot wait for God's timing, or trust what He is doing, but instead choose to do things our way, then we are making idols. God's words in Jeremiah 2:13 cut me to the heart:

> For my people have committed two evils; they have forsaken me the fountain of living waters, to hew for themselves cisterns, broken cisterns, that can hold no water.

God is the Fountain of Living Water, the only One I need to drink from to quench the thirst of my soul. I can choose to go elsewhere other than God, but these substitutes would only be broken cisterns that would not hold water. I would always be in want of something more. Jesus is the only One who can and will satisfy all the deepest desires of my heart.

Elizabeth Elliot was the wife of martyred missionary, Jim Elliot, who was speared to death by the Auca Indians in Ecuador in 1956. Her love story with Jim Elliot is found in the book *The Shadow of the Almighty*. In a radio interview done by Back to the Bible Online entitled, "Waiting on God, Not a Mate," Elizabeth shared her perspective on the issue of waiting. She said:

> Do you believe that God knows how to give you a husband or a wife at the right time? If you were a man, I would ask, "Are you aggressively seeking the will of God in this area?" If you were a woman, I would say to you, "Are you waiting patiently for God's will? Not for a man, but for God Himself?"
>
> **All you have, remember, is today.** You might be dead tomorrow. We could all be raptured. We do not know what a day may bring forth. So it's in this present moment that God is asking you to trust Him. Can you do that until the sun goes down? He is not asking you to trust Him for the next twenty years. He is only giving you today. It is this day and only this day in which you can glorify Him, because the past is gone and the future is not here yet. We don't know what the future holds, but we do know Who holds the future.[5]

Elizabeth Elliot knew quite well about waiting on the Lord. She and Jim loved each other deeply but Jim would not ask her to marry him for some years because he knew God had called him on a mission to Ecuador. He felt he needed an undistracted time in the field and so, did not ask Elizabeth to wait. She, on the other hand, waited for years for Jim to propose marriage. When finally he did and they got married, they only had about two years together until Jim was speared to death by the Auca Indians. The natives had mistakenly thought Jim was a cannibal. Elizabeth knew what it meant to wait on God and trust Him for the desires of her heart.

Waiting in Hope

Lamentations 3: 22-26 says:

> The Lord's loving kindness indeed never ceases. For His compassions never fail. They are new every morning; Great is Your faithfulness. "The Lord is my portion," says my soul, "Therefore I have hope in Him." The Lord is good to those who wait for Him, to the person who seeks Him. It is good that he waits silently for the salvation of the Lord.

---

[5] This radio interview is part of *"Gateway to Joy,"* a production of Back to the Bible Radio Program. It can be accessed online at http://www.backtothebible.org/index.php/Gateway- to-Joy/Waiting-on-God-Not-a-Mate.html (Last Accessed July 10, 2011).

God used this passage when I was struggling through and figuring out what waiting on God meant for me in connection with waiting for Paul, or, more appropriately, waiting for a husband. I had to find out what this meant. I hung on to those promises that assured me that God rewards those who wait. God is good to those who seek Him and hope and wait silently on Him. But how does one do that in the midst of pain and uncertainty? I've found that waiting on the Lord involves three things: hoping in Him (v. 24); seeking Him (v. 25); and waiting silently for Him and for His salvation expectation and desire for a certain thing to happen. John Piper describes biblical hope as:

> A confident expectation and desire for something good in the future. Biblical hope not only desires something good for the future; it expects it to happen. And it not only expects it to happen; it is confident that it will happen. There is a moral certainty that the good we expect and desire will be done.[6]

The posture of a hopeful heart is much like the mother who is confident that, through her groans and painful contractions, something worth struggling for will come out. We Christians can have this kind of expectant heart because of the character of the One upon Whom we wait.

As I looked for many articles about waiting on the Lord, I read and liked this article by J. Hampton Keathley and he explicitly explains that waiting is as sure as the sunrise.

> ...Waiting is fundamentally wrapped up with knowing, trusting, and believing in the Lord and His person (His character) and in His promises. The ability to wait on the Lord stems from being confident and focused on who God is and on what God is doing. It means confidence in God's person: confidence in His wisdom, love, timing, understanding of our situation and that of the world. It means knowing and trusting in God's principles, promises, purposes, and power.[7]

---

[6] John Piper, *"What Is Hope?"* (April 6, 1986), http://www.desiringgod.org/resource library/ sermons/what-is-hope (Last Accessed July 10, 2011).
[7] J. Hampton Keathley III, *"Waiting Silently for Him, Waiting on the Lord,"* http://bible.org/article/waiting-lord (Last Accessed July 10, 2011)

I can wait because my waiting is not based on an empty promise from someone I don't know, but because I'm waiting on Someone I can trust, and whose character I know, the assurance that He is good keeps me eagerly waiting.

Wait Seekingly

My waiting, as Lamentations 3:25 says, should not be a passive waiting. Because "the Lord is good to those who wait for Him, to the person who seeks Him," there is a movement on my part to intentionally seek God and spend all my energies seeking Him.

Again John Piper writes:

> The heavens are telling the glory of God. So we can seek him through that. He reveals himself in his word. So we can seek him through that. He shows himself to us in the evidences of grace in other people. So we can seek him through that. The seeking is the conscious effort to get through the natural means to God himself—to constantly set our minds toward God in all our experiences, to direct our minds and hearts toward him through the means of his revelation. This is what seeking God means. When we enter God's waiting room we are not to just sit as one might in the doctor's chair. Rather, we need to spend time seeking Him. This means: **Time in the Word** studying, seeking answers, and claiming God's promises; **Time in prayer** praying about the issues, praying for wisdom and discernment; **Time meditating on who God is,** what He is wanting to do in us and through us, and on what we need to do by way of answers and direction. Included in this might be our need to examine and evaluate our motives and attitudes, our values and priorities, and our goals and objectives in life.[8]

Wait Silently

The last part about waiting also meant waiting silently. When one is silent, one does not make any sound, one does not speak or express anything aloud. Waiting silently is never easy. I am more prone to

[8] Piper, *"What Is Hope?"*

complain and whine. Waiting silently presents a picture of rest and trust while deep prayer goes on in the heart.

For me it meant silently praying, "Show Yourself to me, God. In my deep pain and frustration, let me get to know You more. Let me understand what You mean when You say You are good to me. That You are enough and can fill the longings of my soul. Manifest yourself to me, Lord. Please calm my heart. Embrace me and wrap Your arms around me."

It meant deeply grieving over the man who would never be mine. As I embraced this pain, my heart rested. My soul was at peace because it was anchored on the truth that God in his goodness did not want me to marry Paul.

I was no longer spinning and moving about, trying everything to fill my longings. God knew my longings and that was enough. In the depth of my hurt and confusion about Paul, I prayed;

> *"In my waiting, God, You are there. I will silence my heart and rest and know You more. In my pain, You are there. I resolve that even if I don't understand all these things that are happening, or why, I will give you my unreserved trust."*

Journaling my Thoughts

★ What does it mean for you to hope, seek, and wait silently on the Lord?

★ Why do you think is it so difficult to wait on God?

★ What is He inviting you to do, or be, as you wait?

★ A simple prayer of trust as we wait on the Lord can be, ***"Lord, walk this lonely road with me. Hold my hand, hug me tight, and be to me what no one else can be at this moment."*** Spend a few moments to say this to God, then remain in silence for some unhurried time.

★ Write your letter and your prayer to God here.

G
Y!
f
t

e-Dating, etc.

CHAPTER SEVEN

7 e-Dating, etc.

A very concerned, loving couple from the US sincerely believed they had to do something about all the single men and women in Philippine Campus Crusade for Christ (PCCC). Their hypothesis was that we singles were just not "out there" enough. We were not doing anything to get ourselves married. So this couple decided to give all of us singles a book by Henry Cloud, *How to Have More Dates and Keep Them*. Dr. Cloud in his book encourages readers to see dating in a whole different light, taking the pressure off them by counseling them to date in order to genuinely know more about the other person, and also know about themselves. According to Dr. Cloud, dating should be used as an opportunity to love and serve others.

I was amused by the different reactions of the single men and women upon receiving the book. I was skeptical, but gratefully received the book and went on to read it. What I got out of it was, "A girl should get out there more, so that she can have more dates," and "it's ok to go online and get to know people from online Christian dating websites." I have always been wary about online dating because it seemed risky to me. I also thought it was only for the "desperate." But I followed the book's advice anyway.

"If I perish, I perish!"

I went online and my sister signed me up for a Christian online dating website. Out of the many men introduced to me, I noticed Michael.

Michael seemed very nice and he sounded conservative and very proper, which made me feel quite safe with him. We went through the process and exchanged emails. After a month, he said he wanted to call me. My heart leaped with excitement and terror. I felt quite safe conversing with him through emails, but now, to actually talk to him? See, this is the thing about online dating stuff: you feel safe while you're anonymous, but once they ask to call or meet with you, you need to decide whether or not you want to go deeper into a relationship. It had been a long time since I allowed a man into my life and let him know me, but I had to echo what Queen Esther said, "If I perish, I perish!" So I resolved to be vulnerable with this man.

He turned out to be a good person. If it were a game of black jack, I would call it GOOD and would have won the game! After about two phone calls from Europe where he was at that time, he said he wanted to meet me. I thought, "Oh my, ok I've got to do this, there's no turning back!"

He Drove 22 Hours To See Me!

One morning in October, I happened to be in the US for some trainings and Michael came to meet me for the first time at my friend Lesley's house in Seattle. He drove 22 hours to get there. Yes, you read that right! Twenty-two hours from the Midwest to Seattle. That was one major plus point for him!

It was a very good first date. He was a handsome 53-year-old, never-been-married Caucasian. My friend Lesley was the one who was most thrilled over him. It was funny that she and her husband were the ones serving us coffee and making sure Michael felt at home. He was quiet, reserved and very mild-mannered. Lesley and I would laugh about how shocked he probably was to see how loud we sounded to him. We went out for two days then I had to go to Oregon and he had to drive the 22 hours back home!

We continued emailing and talking on Skype during the four months that followed. Then one day, I told him I would be in Vancouver in February for training and he asked to come and see me again. Of course I was happy that he asked. Michael seemed like a very steady, loyal person. He said he had had some relationships in the past but the last one left him wounded after the girl left him. An alarm went off in my brain initially and I wondered why a woman would leave such a seemingly nice man for another.

We saw each other on weekends. He would fly straight from work to Vancouver on a Saturday to see me and return home on a Sunday. It was clear that he put in a lot of time and effort to be with me but it also made me wonder how this relationship could be sustained considering the time and distance between us. I also realized that because my love language was quality time, his coming in and out like that made me feel I wanted more from him.

"So, What Are We Doing, Michael?"

At first, we were excited to get together again, but when we began to talk more seriously, I had to ask, "So, what are we doing, Michael?" We were both mature individuals and I was about to leave again for Asia. I wanted to know if this relationship was something I could seriously ask God for. I was hoping he would say, "You know, I don't know and am not sure about my life, but I would like to pursue you and pray with you about this relationship."

But instead he answered, "I don't know. We have two very different worlds and our lives seem to be too far apart." Then he went on about how he didn't know his direction at that time. He was living temporarily with his mother after 20 years of living alone as an industrial tourist, and after switching to a job he did not like. That made me really sad. I realized that we were not on the same page. I thought that because we had met on an online dating site, it meant we were both open for a serious relationship. It turned out that I was ready but he was not.

In my frustration, I wanted to ask, "So why are you even here? Why do you spend all this time and money to come here?" No, I didn't say those words, but I surely thought of them!

It left me all confused but we prayed together and he said he would figure out his life with God and then we would talk again.

One Last Time

I struggled in my heart about where this relationship was going. At the same time, a movie titled "He's Just Not That Into You" came out. As I watched that film, I thought, "Okay, I get it. He's just not that into me!" But I still wanted to know and hear it from him. Maybe, somehow, in the inner recesses of my heart I still kept the hope that this relationship could work.

In the months that followed, we continued to communicate. Then in February the next year, I tried one last time to give Michael a chance to see me, and I think he did try. He said he was coming to see me on Valentine's Day. I was in Texas then. I got excited. My Texan hosts and even their dog Lily were all excited for me. Knowing he loved jazz music, I took time to pick out a classical CD of all jazz legends to give to him as a present. When Valentine's Day came, I got a call from Michael. He said he could not come. He was sick, had major headaches and chills, and couldn't get up from bed so he could not drive four hours down to come and see me.

My heart dropped. I felt it was a clear confirmation of what I feared all along.

Disappointment With God

I cried that Valentine's Day, not necessarily because of Michael. I think I knew he was gone and that I lost him one year ago on that February day in Vancouver. My tears were more because I was disappointed with God.

I told God, "I get it! I get the point! I get what You have been telling me all along!" God had been telling me for a whole year that Michael was not the best man for me. Still I said, "But why did You let me go through all that if he wasn't one person I could consider? Why would You let me meet Michael only to set me up for disappointment, and then do nothing about it?" I cried, "I am disappointed in You, God, because You did not make him want me. I am disappointed in You for making me even think I could hope."

You see, I realize now that it probably did not have to be Michael *per se*. It could have been any other man and I would have said the same. I realized that after my experience with Paul it took a lot of effort on my part to open my heart and make myself vulnerable again before another man. It was difficult for me to hope again, yet as an act of faith, I did. I opened my heart only to have myself set up for more hurt and pain.

As I always react when I'm hurt, I got angry. Angry at myself because I was stupid enough to agree with that couple to read their book. I was angry because I allowed myself to be vulnerable. Being hard-hearted was easier. It prevented me from getting hurt. I was angry with Michael because I thought he was not courageous enough to commit himself to another. I was angry with God because maybe there really was something wrong with me, because I frightened men away and He made me this way. I told myself, "I am done with men!"

Finding The True Lover Of My Soul

Yet in my anger, I tried hard to find the real sadness that gripped my heart. I grieved because, again, I didn't have what I longed for. Honestly, at that time, I longed for a man to pursue my heart and want me. But no man did.

In my disappointment, I turned to the True Lover of my soul and allowed Him to comfort me as I cried. I allowed myself to grieve about having lost a potential relationship. I guess I will never understand what went wrong, but I believe I didn't need to.

A dear 70-plus-year-old lady friend of mine who committed to pray during the time I was going out with Michael, wrote me an email. She said:

> *Dear Orpah, I can understand your concern about Michael. I have to confess that I don't see how there can be a deep relationship with someone who comes in for just a day or so, and who leads such a different lifestyle and really does not know about his commitment to the Lord. And you have such a wonderful outreach ministry that the Lord has given you. Do you really want to give that up? If the Lord wants you to have a partner, He will provide one. Trust Him, but*

don't take second best. Am I being too bold saying that? I am thinking of you and I want the best for you. We love you and pray for you.

Sarah

These were truthful and loving words for my soul. I realize now that this experience was all for me. God wanted me to see that He was enough. I know He wanted me to continue to give my heart and be vulnerable. Though he allowed me to be hurt, He assured me that things would be okay because He was there.

No Good Thing Will He Withhold

As I wept, I told God, "I don't want to harden my heart. I want my heart to be alive and feel the pain because it draws me to You." God reminded me that part of His goodness is not always giving me what I want.

Psalm 84:11 says:

> For the LORD God is a sun and shield; the LORD gives grace and glory; No good thing does He withhold from those who walk uprightly.

If God is good, and if I understand the meaning of good according to my computer dictionary, then it means God wants me to have something that is for my benefit. It also means that God in His goodness wants me to have the things that He desires and which He approves. He wants me to have something that will give both Him and me pleasure, enjoyment and satisfaction. It means He is good and has my best interest at heart. Nothing slips past Him.

If He means it when He says, "He will not withhold any good thing from me as I walk uprightly," then, withholding what I thought was a seemingly good man for me was still part of His goodness. This is something that's quite hard for me to receive sometimes, but when I finally embraced this truth, it gave me peace, and excitement that the best from God is yet to come!

On any other day, I would probably have erased the existence of Michael from my life for what he did, or more appropriately, for what he did not do. But then I remembered that I had resolved to live with a heart that was alive and not hardened by anger. I wanted to be able to feel the pain of relationships and still be willing to give my heart and soul to others.

I opted to stay as friends with Michael. This was part of my choice to live vulnerably. I decided I would continue to email him my personal and ministry updates. I would greet him on his birthday and on Christmas, and send him messages to encourage him, and trust God for the best for him. Yes, Michael and I are still friends and text mates. Sometime after that fateful Valentine's Day, I mailed my present to Michael. I hope he enjoys listening to all that jazz!

The morning of the day that Michael stood me up, I got a huge bouquet of flowers from my Texan hosts. The card said that Valentine's Day was not just for husbands and boyfriends but also for friends who loved me. They didn't know yet what Michael had said, but even in the midst of my grieving at that time, those flowers and words were enough to make my heart full.

You ask me if I would go online and date again?

Today, I would say, "YES!"

Next date please?

Journaling my Thoughts

★ Are you or have you ever been in an e-dating relationship? What was/is that experience like for you?

★ What do you understand about the goodness of God? What does it look like to you?

★ What do you think is God withholding from you right now? Can you believe that this situation is still part of God's goodness towards you? In what way?

★ What does it mean for you to rest in the goodness of God?

★ Write your letter and your prayer to God here.

You're 50?! And You're Still Single?!

CHAPTER EIGHT

8 You're 50? And You're Still Single?

From My Journal

Today, I turn the Big 50! It comes with all the stuff that goes with being a fifty-year-old lady... peri-menopause, bulges everywhere except where you want them, sagging cheeks, and a chin that doubles itself. But hey, this is what it looks like to be half a century old! That's 18,250 days spent and gone!

But today, I'm actually excited to start another half-century altogether! When I was a teenager, the concept of being 50 years old was way beyond what I could imagine. But today, I say, "Huh? Who would even think I'm 50?" I don't feel many aches and pains yet, nor do I look fiftyish. But I'm sure very soon all these signs of aging will be more conspicuous and I will certainly look my age. I will then have to resign myself to reality and say, 'Orpah, deal with it!'

Today I have a choice. I can either sulk over being 50 and husbandless, or I can celebrate life in its fullness and declare what a gift it is to be alive at my age.

Well, I choose to do the latter!

Fun '70s Theme Birthday Party

I grew up with '70s music and have loved the colorful flower power era as far back as I can remember, so I decided I was going to celebrate 50 good years by having a '70s music theme party! What a major production it was!

First, to refresh my memory of what we wore in the '70s, I had to Google '70s fashion, and chose one that liked. It was a pink blouse and pants outfit with a flowered chaleco and a matching beret. Just perfect! So off I went to Kamuning market and hunted down a fabric. I found a deep gold spandex that I fell in love with and a screaming orange printed cotton cloth for the vest. I asked around for a seamstress, found one, and quickly had it made just for the event. To complete my look, my friend Verna, an in-demand make-up artist for a leading cosmetics company, offered to do my '70s make up with matching mile-long false eye lashes and gold dust on my face. On the night of my birthday, I had flower power, clogs, butterfly sleeves, yellow bell-bottoms and sunflowers on my hair!

On the eve of my birthday, I was agog over preparations for the venue. My favorite single lady friends, Malou, Boots and Lilian, helped me decorate the place with groovy '70s paraphernalia. We hung swags of yellow, orange and bright colored cloths from the ceiling to the floor and attached vinyl records to them. Glitter on the walls, colorful balloons on stage, and posters of scenes from the '70s filled the place.

I hired a '70's music band that delivered great music for a song. That was only the first of many best deals of the night. Friends helped to spice up the evening. Vie Cesar-Reyes, my good friend from high school, whom I've dubbed the Coffee Queen of the Philippines, set up her coffee booth and treated us all to overflowing Eighteen Days Coffee@, including the most expensive coffee in the world from the civet mongoose - Alamid coffee@! Jenny Sy gave us a spread of her delicious pastas using her famous Clara Ole@ sauces for everybody to enjoy. Cake Shack@ owned by my friend Genine Garcia and designer Bea Bernardo set up a beautiful psychedelic dessert table laden with three fondant cakes with matching groovy fondant afro-haired centerpiece doll, iced cupcakes, jello on spoons, and candy-sprinkled chocolate lollipops. Talk about sugar high and sensory overload!

I invited all of the most significant people in my life—my family, good friends, disciples in the artists' ministry and special ministry partners—and we danced to the music of The Stylistics, Fifth Dimension, Earth Wind and Fire, and Abba, plus a never-ending medley of disco, rock, and swing music. At one point, we all took to the dance floor as a group and, led by my friend and former Ballet Philippines artistic director—and one of the best dancers I know—Ramon Victoria, we swung the night away to the beat of...what else but..."Dancing Queen!"

Filipino hit makers themselves who were my guests sang authentic '70s hits. The original jazz diva, Louie Reyes, happened to be in town and willingly belted out my favorite Seawind song, "Follow Your Road." She and Ray-An Fuentes, another '70s icon, then did a famous Filipino hit, "Umagang Kay Ganda" that brought the house down. Later in the evening, Kuh Ledesma, the Philippines' finest pop diva, fresh from her concert, caught up with us and sang, "I Will Survive." As the birthday celebrator, I was delighted to see these famous friends of mine in my party jamming, doing all these impromptu numbers and simply having fun. We all had fun as we danced…danced…danced the night away. To end the evening, all of them prayed for me and blessed and encouraged me with words of affirmation as I faced the next 50 years of my life. What a fun, fun birthday celebration it was!

Having fun is a commitment I made many years ago because I wanted to make a statement that we single women can be wonderful Christian models of blessedness to younger men and women. I wanted my nephews and nieces to remember me as the coolest Auntie Orpah they'd ever had. True enough, my nephew Daniel Darwin unashamedly declared in my party, "I want you all to know that my cousins and I all got our craziness directly from Auntie Pah!" Ha! Ha! What a compliment!

Fun Being An Aunt

Since I've never experienced having children, my nephews and nieces filled up this longing for children of my own. When they were all very young, I enjoyed entering their worlds. I had five nephews first before my first niece came, so I had a chance to be completely there for the boys. I would dig up any mound on the earth just to look for a slug, worm, or whatever it was they wanted to see under the rocks and dirt. I would climb any tree with them or dissect a caterpillar or go out into the garage with heavily loaded water guns and get screaming wet—doing all these just before dinner.

On a whim, I emailed my nephews and nieces to ask them to write a paragraph or two about what they would never forget in their times with me as their Auntie Pah. I was quite surprised about what they wrote and how diverse their memories are of our crazy times together. Well, I'll let them tell you themselves.

From Camille Ruth

Back when we cousins were all around the ages of five to ten, Auntie Pah created what she called the "Wormie-wormy." This "Wormie-wormy" was a code-word that was spoken mere moments before Auntie Pah would suddenly launch into an all-out tickling attack on all of us and then we'd all get into the rumble-tumble of giggles and laughter.

We've always known her to be a constant source of high-pitched laughter, screaming and joy during our family reunions. Despite her busy traveling schedule every year, Auntie Pah always prioritizes her family, us, first. Her devotion to my grandparents in caring for them and visiting them is something that we all admire. Every year, she would go off to travel for a few weeks to a few months and come back with all of her precious pasalubongs[9] *for her nieces and nephews. She has always been the most generous one in the family during Christmas reunions. She never hesitates to spoil the ones that she loves.*

Auntie Pah has always loved us fiercely. You can see it in the way she is protective of us whenever there is a new girlfriend that is introduced in family reunions by my male cousins. You can see it in the way that she looks at us with pride whenever we achieve our little accomplishments in life. You can see it in the way that she puts a lot of effort into the little things that make our family reunion times more fun and wild. We all know that Auntie Pah is a very intelligent, independent and tenacious woman but we, her nephews and nieces, will always know her for her crazy side that never ceases to love us, no matter who we are and who we will be.

From Hesed Faith

I remember when I was just about nine and I went to Auntie Pah's house. It was the first time that my parents permitted me to go to her

[9] *Pasalubong* is the Filipino word for "coming home gifts."

house to stay overnight. I wasn't expecting anything that's why I was surprised to know that we were going to make bracelets and earrings out of beads and strings that Auntie Pah prepared for me and my only female cousin Ate Camille. It was a girls' night out and it was extremely fun. I brought the teddy bear and the Bible Auntie Pah bought me for Christmas that year. And then we watched a movie. After that Auntie Pah told us Bible stories and we went to bed. It was an enlightening experience for me as a child because I knew that I have people around me to trust and to learn from.

Then, there was a time when Auntie Pah stayed at our place for a whole year. She taught me how to cook without having the smell of garlic in my hands, a technique that only a few knew. She also taught me how to be a lady with good manners which she had learned when she was little that I as a child had never learned. She cooks real good food that would make your mouth water, it's her language of love—cooking good food to her loved ones so that they may enjoy it—I bet she got that from my grandmother who also cooks so well!

I will never forget the time when Starr, her beautiful golden retriever, was with us and Starr had a long stick in her mouth. Starr was running around hitting people with that stick and her tail wagging like crazy and Auntie Pah ran with us too, all around my brother's room. We had a video experiment that we would make the stick look like a light saber, the one in Star Wars and after making it look like it, we entitled the video, Starr Wars. It was a crazy yet fun experience with her, my brother and of course Starry.

From Joel Allan

I'd say the most fun I had with you, Auntie Pah, was when you invited all of us cousins over for a sleepover one night way back in like 2006 I think. It was when you first got your golden retriever, Starr, and we watched movies and hung out and played with the doggies. I remember it was the last sleepover we all had together in your house in Frisco and it was also kind of a good bye for Daniel (before he left for New York to study college). It was fun to hang out and watch movies with you and just be together. Talking about life was also always very nourishing to me back then and I really appreciate that.

From Michael

I have always known my auntie to be one of the funniest, craziest (in a good way), and most interesting person I have known in my life. Ever since I was little, Auntie Pah was always known to be the aunt who was to entertain and cheer up everyone always. There have been many times in which she has shown such great enthusiasm and happiness in a certain event. One of the times I could remember is whenever Christmas Day comes up and our relatives and families meet up as a clan, Auntie Pah would always like to sing and laugh so much that she could make the whole household resonate with exuberance. This is one of the greatest displays and memories I would have of my aunt where she would exhibit a specialty that only some people in this world have, namely the specialty of giving off a warmth and enjoyment that everyone around her can share. That is why I can always look up to her as an aunt who becomes a model of inspiration to everyone.

It is always fun being an Aunt. I like it much better than being a mom because I can always return my nephews and nieces back to their parents at the end of the day!

We Enter And Get Involved With Life

Luci Swindoll, in her book *Wide my World, Narrow my Bed*, said:

> The happiest single people I know are those who are involved with life, not standing on the sidelines, enduring their plight, waiting for something better to come along. In fact the happiest people I know, in general, are those actively engaged in living, entering into the rhythm of life.[10]

Luci Swindoll is right. We enter and get involved with life. One of my real small joys as a single individual is ministering to people by inviting them over to my home. I take time to cook and pour in all the love and passion I have for them in the food I make. I enjoy cooking dinners, breakfast, or just baking something for friends. I have adopted a habit that I got from a sweet girlfriend who said that every time she cooks or bakes, she prays that whoever eats her cakes will be blessed!

---

[10] Luci Swindoll, *Wide my World, Narrow my Bed* (Portland, OR: Multnomah Press, 1982), 36.

These are often families or younger men and women and missionaries from my organization. I express my love for them by coming up with a major production of wonderful food! I love feeding those I love!

In the Philippines, Thanksgiving Day is not celebrated with as much flourish as it is in the USA. There was one Thanksgiving Day though that I celebrated while in the US, and I watched and helped my sister come up with a whole production of all the dishes they would make for Thanksgiving. I resolved that day that when I came home to my country, I would make sure my friends would experience Thanksgiving Day the way they do in America.

The next year, I eagerly looked forward to Thanksgiving Day, having excitedly dolled up my house with all the fall colors of orange, yellow and green. All the decors from tablecloths to napkins were in these vibrant fall colors. There were plastic or Styrofoam pumpkins and gourds of different sizes, a scarecrow, maple leaves, and acorns, which I brought home from the USA for this occasion. A big part of the fun was doing the stuffed turkey, which I cooked for five hours, and making all the side dishes of cranberry sauce, mashed potatoes, green beans casserole, pineapple yam bake, and corn, and then setting them all on a beautiful table. Then came my favorite part, which was cooking the pecan pie. What great fun it was!

I invited about three families and five single friends to come for Thanksgiving. As part of tradition, I asked someone to give the story of how the first Thanksgiving Day started and all of us appreciated the story behind this beautiful American tradition. Then each one was asked to share one thing they wanted to thank God for in the past year. We all ate with joy and awe at this wonderful tradition that I promised to adopt ever year. Turkey was great and everyone was stuffed by the end of the evening. It was a huge success! I was a tired, happy and beautiful host!

It was only upon turning 50 that I ventured on death-defying rides and trips like going whitewater rafting in Cagayan De Oro in Southern Philippines and taking a ride on the longest zip line in Asia found in Dahilayan Park in Bukidnon, Philippines. I have always clung to the motto of trying anything once. I still love going mountain climbing. My next goals are Mt. Pulag in Northern Philippines, and Mt. Apo, our country's highest peak found in the South. Plus I want to experience the rain forest and take a trip down the Amazon River!

Then there's singing. The gladdest thing for me is when we sing to people and give joy through our songs and music. When I was deciding what to take up in college, I had to choose between Veterinary Medicine and voice at the U.P. College of Music. I chose Vet. Med. but the passion to sing and give hope to people through music has always been in my veins. I helped start a music ministry called Windsong, in the University of the Philippines College of Music in 1985 and until now this ministry teaches churches and other organizations to use music for the expansion of God's kingdom.

In my former church, I put together a singing group called Masterpiece and we used music to share the gospel to groups and individuals. One of our traditions at Christmastime was visiting dialysis patients at the National Kidney Center to sing and share with them about the love and forgiveness of Jesus through music. It was difficult to see people suffering but we were grateful for the chance, though small, to give hope and joy through music.

More than at any time, I am most sensitive to people who are suffering and in pain, whether physically or emotionally. Oftentimes I can't offer any words except to be there and just sit with them in silence and grieve with them. Listening to them always helps heal. But oftentimes, God gives me wisdom to be spontaneous and ask them to go do something crazy and fun that will help them in their healing too.

Have Fun, Not for Escape

My capacity for fun and joyful experiences is sometimes enough to keep me sane in difficult times. However I have promised myself never to use it as escape from things that oftentimes require painful authenticity. I've promised myself it's okay to have fun but to not forget the idiosyncrasies of being single.

People know that I do not hide my age nor do I dread getting older. In fact, I see it as God's bonus for me. Every year, I learn many things about myself that make me wiser and more mature, especially in my relationships with men and women, and in my relationship with God.

So, yes, I'm 50 and I'm still single, but hey! I'm having fun!

Journaling my Thoughts

★ List down 10 things about your being single today that you can thank God for.

1.
2.
3.
4.
5.
6.
7.
8.
9.
10.

★ Write down ten fun things that you know you have the capacity to do as a single person. What keeps you from doing them? *(Get your planner now and start scheduling when you want to do the first three things in your list. List others as your year unfolds.)*

1.
2.
3.
4.
5.
6.
7.
8.
9.
10.

★ How would you model a single woman's life of fun and laughter?

★ Write your letter and your prayer to God here.

NEGLECT
ABUSE
NEGLECT
ABUSE
NEGLECT
ABUSE
ABUSE

Anatomy of a Wounded Heart

CHAPTER NINE

9 Anatomy of a Wounded Heart

My mother was an English teacher. She taught us that if we were to speak English we should speak it properly or not at all. *Nanay* played the piano and taught the church choir. I sang in the choir with her as early as I could remember. My *Nanay* was designed by God to be the best hostess in our home. She always made sure there was food ready for any church member who might come any time of the day. That's why my siblings and I didn't think that we were poor growing up. We always had food on the table. *Nanay* was the one who influenced us most about propriety and made sure we behaved well around other people by being respectful, obedient, and proper in our ways.

Nanay exposed us to a huge array of music. She would bring me to operas and stage plays at the Cultural Center of the Philippines. She exposed us to classical and modern music, folk songs, and beautiful hymns. She has a wonderful ear for music. If you were a musician, she could be your best fan or your worst critic. I appreciate *Nanay* because if not for her, we would not have developed our musical talents. However, because we were a poor pastor's family, she didn't have time and resources for us to even learn how to play the piano. I still grieve about this sometimes. She encouraged us to develop our voices instead. *Nanay* let us join different glee clubs in school and she was present whenever we had performances during various school events.

Growing up in a pastor's home, we understood early on that we were supposed to be in church every Sunday. My father would normally preach and my mother would play the organ during worship.

Because my *Tatay* was not a leader of a big denomination but was a small church pastor, he spent more time at home. He was more often present at home than my *Nanay* was. As I write this book, they are still alive; *Nanay* is 86 and *Tatay* is 88. I truly value each day they are still with us and I appreciate the legacy of faith they have handed down to my siblings and me.

I am the youngest of four children. My eldest sister is Leah. She is almost like my second mother. I didn't fully realize this until we were in Canada, where we were both training with Hope Alive Counseling. She told me that when I was a little girl, she took me under her wing as her own baby when *Nanay* went to teach in school. That's probably why I gravitate to my sister, Leah, when I have problems. If I had to consult with someone, it would be Leah first, then my other sister Ammi second.

As I mentioned in an earlier chapter, when I was 12, Leah took me to the College Life Fellowship at the University of the Philippines to listen to a speaker, Dr. Bill Bright, who was then Campus Crusade for Christ International President. I was in high school and she was in college. That night of December 14, 1973, Dr. Bright spoke to a group of college students including myself. He made us understand that God loved each one of us and had a wonderful plan for our lives. He said that I needed to receive Christ into my life as my personal Savior and Lord to experience that wonderful plan. I realized that my pastor father couldn't do that for me. This was between God and me. I said, okay that sounds good. I prayed with Dr. Bill Bright and invited Jesus Christ into my life as my personal Savior and Lord. That same night, Leah shared with me the little booklet called *"Four Spiritual Laws"* and everything I did with Dr. Bright that night became more clear. Leah is my real mother in the spiritual sense.

My second sister, Ammi, is our journalist. She loves to talk and write. She has a comment about anything and everything. I thought she was the smartest of us all, because she always had something to say about current events. She and my father read and discussed the newspapers together. I was the quiet one. I didn't like reading; nor did I enjoy keeping up with current events. But she must have fooled me because now I think it's our only brother Lemuel who is the smartest of us all.

My *Koya*[11] Lemuel naturally excelled in class and would have scholarships every year. He was a college scholar at the University of the Philippines College of Medicine while I was just breezing my way through the University of the Philippines College of Veterinary Medicine. He graduated as a scholar while I was just happy to finish college. He is our "human medicine doctor." I needed to make that clear because I'm the animal medicine doctor, remember? We used to have a standing joke in the family that after we had both gotten our medical licenses we would have a sign posted in front of our house that went like this: *"If you are a human patient, call Dr. Lemuel. If you are an animal patient, call Dr. Orpah!"*

Koya Lemuel was my playmate. We built houses on trees, played with our dogs, climbed rooftops, aimed at trees with our slingshots and toy guns. Unfortunately, because my brother needed a playmate, most of my games were games for boys. I would always be dirty at play. I never had a doll when I was young but I had one stuffed toy dog named Jondi.

I remember my mother saying, "When Orpah was born we were hoping to have another boy. When she came out, the nurse brought her in and told me my baby was a girl and I said, 'Oh no, that's a mistake, she should have been a boy!'"

She would go on to say, "You see, I have three girls. The two older girls, Leah and Ammi—I don't let them play outside our compound because they need looking after. But you see that Orpah? I just let her go, she likes to play outside with the dogs and climb trees. She plays with her brother and I know she's okay. She's not easily hurt, she can take care of herself."

When we were little kids, my father would bring us around the city of Manila and let us ride the public utility vehicle called jeepney.[12]

---

[11] *Koya*, pronounced |koi-uh| and more commonly spelled "Kuya," is the Filipino word for "elder brother."

[12] Jeepneys started out as American surplus military jeeps left behind after WWII and later reconfigured, through Filipino ingenuity, to become the most popular means of public transportation in the Philippines. They are now long-bodied, flamboyantly decorated vehicles where passengers sit side by side and face to face with each other.

Tatay would strike a conversation with anyone inside the jeepney and introduce the three of us girls to the passengers. He would point to my sister Leah and say, "Oh, this is my Miss Universe!" Then he would point to Ammi and say, "This one is my Miss World!" And then pointing to me, he would say, "And this last one is my Miss International! These are my most beautiful daughters." Of course the people in the jeep would smile and had no choice but to agree! *Koya* Lemuel was already special because he was the only boy.

As the youngest, I was the baby of the family. During family crises, my older siblings would usually take charge. Leah would try to solve the crisis; Ammi would talk about the situation and then move to take action; and Lemuel would help my sisters and father when needed. They would all tell me to stay on the side and wait till everything was over. I didn't have to do or say anything. I looked around and observed things as they played out. My siblings would let me join in only when the crisis was over or when they desperately needed another hand.

When I took a course in Biblical Counseling, our teacher informed us about some findings in Psychology regarding sibling relationships. He said that there is usually a pattern in the way siblings react to a crisis. One normally takes charge, another solves the problem, another appeases people, and another one hides. I was the one who would hide.

My hiding was not necessarily physical. But I would hide my fear of not knowing what was going on. I mostly hid my confusion and pretended I understood everything. I had no words to my emotions. I was not asked if I was afraid or if I was confused about what was going on. I would be quiet and keep my fear in silence. I would play out the events in my mind and try to figure out things on my own. When I could not understand them, I would get angry.

In the book she co-wrote with her husband John, Stasi Eldredge says, "Shame causes us to hide. We are afraid of being truly seen and so we hide our truest selves and offer only what we believe is wanted. If we are a dominating kind of woman, we offer our "expertise". If we are a desolate kind of woman, we offer our "service." We are silent and do not say what we see or know when it is different from what others are saying, because we think we must be wrong. We refuse to bring the weight of our lives that God has made us to be, to bear on others out of a fear of being rejected."[13]

In the next parts of this chapter, I will write about my parents. My goal is not to dishonor them but to use our story to help others think through their own personal issues. I acknowledge that *Tatay* and *Nanay* are good, godly parents and yet they are also flawed and sinful as all parents are. They parented me in the way they knew best and I appreciate them very much.

Tatay and Nanay's Parenting Style

My parents' parenting style was entirely different from the way they related to each other as a married couple. They loved us their children to bits, but were oblivious to the dysfunctional way they related to each other. Their marital relationship affected me as a person. It also affected the way I related to men.

My *Tatay* was orphaned at an early age. He lost his mother when he was a year old, and his father when he was in sixth grade. His two elder sisters and an aunt raised and seemed to have spoiled him. He hardly had any models of a good father or of a loving, caring mother. He was neglected in many ways and had to fend for himself even at a very young age. My mother would often complain that my father had no finesse in eating, and was very indiscreet in speaking. I think it was because my father had lived through a rough childhood.

My mother on the other hand had a loving and thoughtful father but an abusive mother. My mother's father was a kind, gentle and generous person who was protective of his daughter. My *Nanay* probably expected *Tatay* to be like her father, but *Tatay* turned out to be the exact opposite. *Tatay* was careless with his hurtful words. He was stingy with money and was not a generous giver. He was not affectionate at all or thoughtful towards our mother and sometimes would even be unkind to some people. This would prove to be a constant source of friction between them, because my mother had been raised to love others, to be kind to the poor, and treat people with respect.

---

[13] John and Stasi Eldredge, *Captivating. Unveiling The Mystery Of A Woman's Soul* (Nashville TN: Thomas Nelson, Inc., 2010), 75.

Whenever my mother was hurt by my father's words and actions, she would act as if nothing happened but would quickly compose herself. She would not let people know that she was deeply hurt. She would show anger toward my father only in front of us, her children. For my mother to elicit a reaction out of my father or to make him do what she wanted, she would have to be very, very angry. In my early years, I saw that my *Nanay* decided anger could be very powerful. It could make people do things for you.

The dynamics at home oftentimes brought confusion to my young brain because I often saw two sides of both my parents. At home, *Nanay* was always angry, worried and verbally abusive towards *Tatay* and sometimes towards us too. But when she was at work (she became a guidance counselor at our High School), or when she related to people at church, the words ascribed to her by her coworkers, churchmates, and even by my own classmates, were "gentle," "kind," and "very loving."

The one good thing about *Tatay* was his devotion towards us, his children. *Tatay* balanced *Nanay*'s abusive words with his encouraging belief in us. He truly cherished us. But there were also times when he would spank some of my siblings even without explanation. As I look back, I realize that these must have been the times when he and *Nanay* were fighting, and they projected their anger towards us.

My *Nanay* had a negative comment on almost anything that *Tatay* did. She very seldom believed in the capabilities of my father. She would emasculate him with words in a way that tore him to pieces. I saw my father crumble and be very desolate at times. As an observer, I became so angry with my father for not fighting back and showing my mother who was stronger and who was in charge. She always ended up being in charge. If only he acted strongly and showed her who was in charge, then maybe she would have shut up.

When all my siblings left home to live alone, I was the last one who saw more of their fights. These would often escalate and the only way to shush my mother was for my father to be very angry and threaten to hit her if she didn't stop. Only then would she calm down, realizing that he did have a capacity to get angry. Unfortunately, sometimes, I find myself behaving in the same way with men. If I don't take a man seriously because I don't believe in him or his capabilities, I test him by poking and goading him to anger. Then I wait to see what happens. When he gets really angry, that's when I stop.

Most of the time, my parents coped with their hurt by giving each other the cold shoulder. They never tried to resolve their issues verbally, but would simply stew in silence. Then when someone resumed the conversation, they both would act like everything was okay. That is, until the next hysterical fight. My father coped with this hot-and-cold war by playing bowling and chess. Sometimes he would come home very late at night hoping not to deal with their issues.

Many friends have expressed their bewilderment about the character of my parents' dynamics. Upon reading about my parents' story, my editor remarked, "I would like to know how a kind and gentle mother turned out to be such an abusive nag, and how a happy, playful father turned out to be such a hard and cold husband."

How indeed? I do not presume to understand exactly what went on, but my hypothesis is that they came to their marriage with many expectations that neither of them could meet, and so they both came away with deep disappointment. They probably expected many things from each other that they had always wanted from their own parents but never or seldom received—love, acceptance, appreciation, self-worth. But over the years, being unable to give what the other needed, each failed to get what they wanted. As time wore on, their level of frustration with each other increased.

They had many unresolved issues coming out of the neglect and abuse they had suffered as children, and maybe even well into their young adulthood, which they re-enacted in their marriage and passed on to us. Somewhere along the way, my mother, having been hurt so many times by her husband, had probably given up praying because she believed she would never see her husband change. I guess the same was true for *Tatay* because every time I confronted both of them to ask why they did what they did to each other, they would fall back on the line, "We have always lived this way, and we will die this way!"

God's Design for Man and Woman

I came to terms with all these when I was taking my counseling course. I learned that God designed us as man and woman who nurture each other in relationships, but we have distorted this design. Medical school taught me that one has to know the normal functions of organs, or their physiology, in order to know why they became sick or pathologic. My teacher George Blake helped me to understand all these when he spoke about what Dr. Larry Crabb said concerning God's original design for men and women. If we know this design, we can then tell where we went wrong in our relationships and how we can set things right.

Blake quotes Dr. Larry Crabb by saying;

> God's design was for man to move in sacrificially, and courageously, risking himself for the well-being of others. But because of the fall of mankind, he now avoids initiating relationships and taking responsibility for them.[14]

In his book, Crabb says,

> Men are called to move into darkness, to keep moving ahead with purpose and strength even when they cannot clearly see the path before them.[15]

And for the woman, Blake has this to say,

> God's design for woman was to be soft and vulnerable, to trust even when there's no reason to, to give and to receive from her man. But because of the fall of mankind she now has to know how best to protect her heart from being damaged by her man.[16]

Stasi Eldredge says,

> So God endows Woman with certain qualities that are essential to relationship, qualities that speak of God. She is inviting. She is vulnerable. She is tender. She embodies mercy. She is also fierce and fiercely devoted...Tender and inviting. Intimate and alluring. Fiercely devoted. Oh yes, our God has a passionate, romantic heart. Just look at Eve.[17]

---

[14] Blake, lecture notes.

[15] Larry Crabb, *The Silence of Adam: Becoming Men of Courage in a World of Chaos* (Grand Rapids, MI: Zondervan Publishing Co.,1995), 61.

[16] Blake, lecture notes.

[17] Eldredge, *Captivating*, 31.

My Thoughts About Men

Unfortunately, when I look at my life, I feel like I am anything but tender and inviting, intimate and alluring. I feel I re-enact many of my parents' situations in my relationships with men. I have thought men to be weak and to have to prove themselves to me first before I could trust them. I have thought men to be not good enough, since the women in my life have been the stronger ones. I am overwhelmed to know how I may have damaged my female soul by being the one who has always had to move courageously, risking for others. I have always made sure that I would not be vulnerable. I have had to take control so that I would not get hurt.

Part of my damage is thinking that men will not come through for me. On my first year in college, I had to register at this university that I had never been to. Because I was a new high school graduate, I did not know what to do to register, and I was afraid to go there on my own. That morning, I was coming down from the stairs when I saw my father lying on the couch, watching TV. I asked him, "*Tatay*, I need to go and register at this college. Can you please come with me?" While on the couch, he said, "No, I will not go with you because the best way for you to learn is by going there on your own. Take a jeepney and ask the drivers, ask the pedicab drivers, and find out for yourself."

I was quite surprised by his answer and wondered why he could not do it, but I thought to myself, "Okay, I will go and look for that school. I need to muster enough courage to do this." I was going to show my father that I could find this school. I asked the jeepney drivers and the pedicab drivers, and eventually found the school. When I got there, I asked the security guards and the people standing around and acted like I knew what I was doing so that people would not take advantage of a freshman like me.

Later in my counseling course, I realized that this disappointment in my father was damaging for me. Because I was very young, I would have felt safer if my father had accompanied me to look for that school. Since he had just been lying there and not doing anything, I felt that he could have easily made an effort to accompany me. He would then have spared me the dread of going to an unknown place, and the anxiety of having to act strong and tough when in fact I was terrified. I also felt uncomfortable asking jeepney drivers and pedicab drivers who were known to make catcalls as girls passed by, and I always feared they would take advantage of my ignorance.

Looking at things from my father's side, I believe that he did this to make me "grow up." He didn't know how badly disappointed I was in him. I could have protested his non-action and persuaded him to get up and go with me but I didn't. He often praised me for my independence because I did things on my own. What he didn't realize was that he was reinforcing my resolve to build a hard outward shell.

Vows I Made As A Young Girl

Unfortunately, this incident made me decide I would never ask him, or any man again, for anything. I concluded that no man would ever do anything for me even if he had the capacity to do so. So I needed to muster enough courage to fend for myself. That resolve damaged my view of men and my dependence on men, and, as I embraced anger and toughness instead of tenderness and vulnerability, it damaged my heart as well.

Somehow I didn't realize I'd made many such resolutions arising from my wounded heart and my impaired view of men. I somehow re-enacted the way my mother treated my father especially in the way she would provoke my father until she got a response. Sometimes, I would say inwardly, "If you are a man and you don't know what you're doing, then please get out of my way so that I can do what I need to do myself. Please don't waste my time because I know I can do things better than you can." Men sense this and so I was never a welcoming person to them.

Aside from my father, the other very significant man in my young life was my male cousin, Abel, who was about ten years older than me. He was taking up Veterinary Medicine at the University of the Philippines. He was very fond of me and loved me as his youngest girl cousin. He was drawn to me because I loved animals, too. He introduced me to the world of horses. Because he was a veterinarian for famous people in the country, I was so proud of him. Abel would bring me to the racetracks and I thoroughly enjoyed watching and beholding these beautiful, majestic equine creatures. He showed me how he did surgical procedures on the horses as they were standing up, and in my six-year old mind, I said, "I want to do that when I grow up!"

Years later, Abel brought me to UP and took out a horse from the barn. "Okay, Orpah," he said, "here are the reins, go and take this horse and ride around the whole UP campus!" So off I went. I was thrilled to take the reins of this beautiful bay horse. I fearlessly rode the huge horse as I crazily raced with the jeepneys on their UP route. I was just a girl of 10 then and I was on that horse all on my own. The jeepney drivers and passengers were all looking at me. I loved the attention and being in control of a huge animal. I was proud that I rode faster than the jeepneys.

One day Abel came home from UP bringing a little white horse named Loser. He figured that since it was time for Loser to retire, I could ride him. He hoisted me atop Loser and said, "Orpah, your goal is to stay on top of the horse. Never let horses know that you are afraid. Make them know that you are the master, otherwise they will master you. This way, they will obey you." With grief in my heart, I am sorry to say that I made this my own personal motto.

At one time he saw me again at home and said, "Orpah, it's time to ride on a horse without the saddle." So he taught me how to clip my thighs against the body of the horse, and hold on to its mane while I kept my balance. Then off I went. Well, you know what happened next. I fell off the horse because I wasn't pressing hard enough with my thighs and because the horse was too big for me. When I fell, Abel congratulated me, "Now you are a rider. All riders fall off a horse."

When he said that, I was on the brink of wanting to cry both from the pain of falling and the pain of failing to do what he wanted. Yet I held back my tears; nothing came out of my mouth. I lost my feminine voice and decided to put on a hard armor so he would not see my pain. I wanted to protest that I was too young, I was just a little girl. Why didn't he protect me from this fall? He shouldn't have made me ride without a saddle because he probably knew this was exactly what would happen. Why didn't he protect me from getting hurt? Why did he want me to be hurt?

Instead of asking if I was hurt and comforting my young heart because I might have been terrified by the fall, all that my cousin Abel said was that now I was a rider. At that time, I had to pick myself up from the dirt, in pain and fear. But something in my heart told me that I had to master those emotions. Something about my female soul died. I was not supposed to show him what I felt because that's what all riders do. From that day on I resolved that I would have no place in my soul for vulnerability. I would harden my heart and be tough.

Stasi Eldredge says,

> The vows we made as children act like a deep seated agreement with the messages of our wounds. 'Fine if that's how it is, then that's how it is. I'll live my life in the following way...' The vows we made acted like a kind of covenant with the messages that came with our deep wounds. Those childhood vows are very dangerous things. We must renounce them. Before we are entirely convinced that they aren't true, we must reject the messages of our wounds. It's a way of unlocking the door to Jesus. Agreements lock the door from the inside. Renouncing the agreement unlocks the door to Him. [18]

Many years later, my relationships with men would affirm that having a tough exterior was always much better. All the men in my life wanted me to be tough and hard. There was no time or reason to be vulnerable. I decided men would not protect me. They would not do things for me even if they could. I could not rely on them to protect my soul.

Sadly, that was the motto of my life for a long time. I didn't like to let people know that I could be hurt, that I was scared and needed help. But you see, I did not know that those parts that I hid were the parts that were most lovely about me as a female. I didn't know I was not able to love well because I kept my heart to myself and didn't give it away. I showed only the hard outer shell. I wasn't around much for people. I made sure that people wouldn't be able to catch me long enough to see what was inside that they might not like—and in that I felt safe.

---

[18] Eldredge, *Captivating,* 102.

Journaling my Thoughts

★ How would you describe your relationship with your mother?

★ With your father?

★ How did your parents relate to each other?

★ What relational dynamic do you think was modeled to you by your parents that affected your relationship with men?

★ What good things do you re-enact in your present relationship with men?

★ What damaging things do you re-enact in your present relationship with men?

★ My way of deadening my heart so as not to get hurt was to get angry and be controlling. How have you deadened your heart so that you would not feel the pain of relationship?

★ Write below your prayer to God about all these:

My Female Heart: Lost and Found!

CHAPTER TEN

10 My Female Heart: Lost and Found!

So, what did it take for me to find my lost feminine soul?

As I said in the previous chapter, all throughout my life I made resolutions not to depend on men. I perfected the art of being in control so that others would not hurt me. Since I showed my heart only to people with whom I felt safe, I was very good at making people think I didn't need them. I did not know how to give or receive from them. In other words, I did not know how to love.

Facing The Truth About Myself

Realizing that my commitment to protect my heart had fractured parts of myself, I undertook a journey to look for my lost feminine soul. The first thing I needed was to face everything that was real and truthful about myself, including those parts. I wrestled with many things about myself. I needed to say, "Orpah, this is what you are really like!" even if I cringed at what I saw. Crabb said,

> The path to maturity begins with an honest look at how we relate. What effect do we have on people? If they had the courage, what would our wives, children and friends tell us about what it is like to be in a relationship with us? [19]

Our professor in counseling class made us ask five significant people in our life to find out what they really thought of us. He said we could ask our roommate, husband, wife, best friend or anyone willing to take

[19] Crabb, *Silence,* 141.

a risk in their relationship with us. "If they tell you what they think," he said, "then that's great. But if they can't tell you what they really think about you, then that tells you something else…"

In the Philippines, we have the privilege of having househelp. I was told, "Go ask your helper what you are like!" Househelp know too much about us that not many people in our world know about. They see our dirty but true stuff. So I asked my helper one morning. After assuring her that I would not kill her (yet), she went on to say, "Orpah, you always shout at me when I make a mistake. You scare me. I also know you love me. But when you're mad, you're really mad."

I want to assure you that she is still alive. But what she said caused me both shame and grief because she told me what I was really like. Of course I asked forgiveness from her and even asked her to courageously tell me or give me a sign to stop if ever I became very angry again, just to let me know… like a Peace sign.

In Montagne d'amour, my friend William pointed out to me, "Orpah, do you know you are so spoiled?" to which I quickly retorted in my brain, "I am not spoiled, I only want my way five times a day!" I may be laughing about these now but what he said made me think. It's true! I was a bit spoiled. I managed to get what I wanted. And if I did not get what I wanted, I made people pay.

Acknowledging what is real and true about myself was the first step to finding my lost female heart. It made me sad and disturbed about the way I dealt with people. This led me to want to change. This set me on the path towards growth.

I realized that I had learned not to speak when I was hurt, so I needed to practice speaking out what I felt—words like "I am sad," "I am hurt," "I am anxious," "I was hurt when you said that!" I had an automatic shut down mechanism in my brain that told me to be quiet and not react. I would store all these feelings inside of me and then get angry because I had no words to my emotions. This was a holdover from my coping behavior as a little girl.

Many of us may have come from abusive backgrounds. Abuse, I am finding out more and more, is a humongous word. The men who were supposed to love and nurture our female hearts wounded us through actions or words that cut deep. Instead of protecting us, they took advantage of our vulnerability. Many of us never knew what it meant to be cherished by a man, so we settled for any man who offered cheap substitutes and we ended up with more neglected needs and unsatisfied longings. Some of you may have had abortions. Instead of facing the truth in order to grieve over the loss of your child, you turned to rage and despair.

In my studies as a Hope Alive Counselor, I found that abuse never happens alone. It is always accompanied by neglect. The many studies made by Dr. Philip Ney, described in his book *Deeply Damaged* [20] and in his website www.messengers2.com, show that persons who suffered from neglect were more prone to abuse. The more abused and neglected they were, the easier it was for them to abort their child. He goes on to say how deeply abortion damages the woman, the man in relationship, and even the babies who survive it. Many have not grieved well over the babies they have lost. This is tragic, since facing the truth about the damages that our hearts sustain is our first step to growth and change.

Facing The Truth About Our Pains And Losses

What I said in the previous chapter about my father may have triggered many things that made you long for a good father. When I wrote about my father's delight in us growing up as women, some of you may have felt pain in knowing you never had a father like that. Some of you may have had fathers who hurt you, not so much with his hands as with his words. You might have had fathers who looked at you, not with delight, but with dismay and disappointment. Some of you probably had fathers who sexually abused you. When we are willing to face the truth about our losses, including the painful experiences of our past, then we are well on our way to finding our lost female soul.

I realized that the best way I could heal was to understand the pain in my life, and its effects on my person and character and how

[20] Philip G. Ney, *Deeply Damaged*, 3rd ed. (Victoria BC: Pioneer Publishing, 1998).

I coped with it. I had to listen to my mentors, study on my own, and read up on my own issues. A huge part of my healing came from my reconciliation with all those who hurt me as well as with those whom I had hurt. Every day I have to choose to offer a heart that is alive and vulnerable and to allow myself to feel the pain of relationship instead of shutting my heart to all that could hurt me.

Learning To Believe That Men Are Good

I needed to learn to believe that there are men who are good and who would be concerned for my good. I needed to learn to entrust my heart to men and to believe that they would not necessarily want to hurt me. I needed to rediscover what it meant to depend on men and believe that they would come through for me. Though they could hurt me, I could still give my heart in relationship to them instead of running away from them. When I do get hurt, I need to be able to speak up and say, "What you did or said, hurt me." I need to learn to bring all of my hurts, and fears about relationships at the feet of Jesus and let Him deal with all these.

I'm still continually learning not to be quick to get angry, but to be quick to look at the real emotion behind my anger. Is it hurt? Is it a small disappointment? Then when I've identified it, I would go to God in prayer and say, *"Lord, what that man did to me, hurt me. It's painful to see he does not have my good at heart. I grieve that this man did not handle my heart well. All my insides are telling me to fight back and make him pay the price, yet I know this is not what you want me to do. Would you please take this hurt and comfort my heart? Help me to express my hurt well so he won't do it again to me or to other women. Help me to reconcile with this man without damaging his soul too. Thank you that you can do this for me."*

Anger - A Hard Façade

Everyday I have to repent of the way I protect my heart from hurt by being angry, or by showing a hard façade just to keep myself in control. I have a long way to go but once in a while I experience small victories in the choices I make, with the help of the One who loves me and is committed to help me find my lost female heart. Sometimes I wonder if I will ever overcome my natural resistance, and become mature.

My counseling mentor once said, "You know you are changing because people will tell you that you are." He's right. Let me tell you of one lady I used to work with. She was my piano accompanist while I led in worship, and we would work together to come up with a praise and worship repertoire. In the few years I was learning to rediscover my female heart, she told me, matter-of-factly, during the end of our rehearsals and from out of the blue: "Orpah, you have not barked at me yet." Then she added that she actually enjoyed our rehearsal and thanked me for my time. I went away grieved because she had told me what I was really like, but I also walked away with joy knowing that I was changing and that there was hope for a woman like me.

All these take a lot of hard work. But I believe I'm finally discovering God's original design for my heart. When I consciously depend on God to change me, I like what I see. I like it when people feel welcome in my life. I like it when they're not scared to come and be in a relationship with me, when they want to know me more and I can offer to them the softness and warmth of a heart that's becoming more in synch with what God wants. And I like it when other people tell me they like what they see, and that what they see is actually beautiful!

Journaling my Thoughts

★ What are you REALLY like? Ask five significant people who will be truthful to you. Commit to not defend yourself.

★ How do you feel about what they have said?

★ Were you ever abused before? How have you sought help about this?

★ Have you ever had an abortion or taken part in one? If so, how do you think did it damage you?

★ How does abuse, neglect, or abortion damage a person?

★ To find out more about abuse, neglect and abortions and how to get help, read up on articles by Dr. Philip G. Ney at www.messengers2.com. You may read ***Deeply Damaged*** and order it online. Anytime you need help, you can contact Hope Alive counselors in the different countries listed on the website.

★ Write your letter and your prayer to God here.

Manipulative & Controlling? Who!? Me!?

CHAPTER ELEVEN

11 Manipulative & Controlling? Who!? Me!?

"Come on, Orpah! Enough already! Stop being sorry for yourself. Someone's got to say ENOUGH to women! And it shouldn't be us men!" These were the words of my favorite teacher and mentor Dr. Philip Ney—who has become a good friend to me—when I told him I was going to write a book on singleness. He continued, "Do you know that there are ten different things that women are more given an advantage of than men? Someone's got to tell them that many women are not married because women want to control men and they want to prove to men that women are better." He expounds on this more in his article, "The Myth of Modern Man."[21]

Enough already! Why don't some of us have a man in our lives? Maybe Philip was right. Many times we want to control men. Before you hunt down Dr. Ney and refute that article, let me show you how we women actually take control.

Manipulative? Yes, I can manipulate. I can control! Dr. Ney defines manipulation thus:

> Manipulation is...trying to get what you want in an indirect dancing, urching,[22] or coercive manner. It occurs when people are afraid to ask for help directly because they suspect rejection.

---

[21] The article can be accessed at http://www.messengers2.com/myth-of-modern-man/ May 7, 2007.

[22] "Urching" is a term we use in Hope Alive group counseling to describe a false face people wear—like acting poor, dirty and pitiable to attract attention and get what they want.

> With manipulation, people can still hope that someday they will obtain what they want,
>
> but if others reject them it is because their technique failed—not because they are unlovable.[23]

We have learned to manipulate because the many things we needed and wanted as a child were not given to us when we asked for them. Significant people in our lives did not listen to us. Nor did they give us the things we needed even when they had the capacity and means to do so. We learned to get the things we wanted in indirect, coercive, and manipulative ways. Unfortunately even now as adults we sometimes still do the same things.[24]

How does one move from being a manipulative, controlling woman to becoming a vulnerable, welcoming, softhearted woman?

Many of these descriptions mostly come from my notes under George and Connie Blake's counseling class. George and Connie were missionaries who lived in Manila for many years and they were used by God to disturb my life in a way that made me want to change.

The most interesting memory I have of the Blakes was during one of George's classes and Connie was sitting right next to me. He spoke to us single women and said, "All you single ladies, you think you are lonely? Well, I have seen the loneliest women in some married women, especially those whose husbands do not move well in their lives." He went on to say, "If you are to marry a man, marry a man who will die for his wife and will model brokenness in the home."[25] George was describing a man who, instead of being passive, risked himself to actively engage the heart of his wife.

I quickly nudged Connie and said, "Where is that man, Connie?" She pointed to her husband and said, "There's one." Then she turned to me and said, "For you, he must be there somewhere!"

---

[23] Philip G. Ney, *Hope Alive Manual* (British Columbia: Pioneer Publishing, 1998), 152.

[24] Ney, Manual, 153-154.

[25] Blake, lecture notes, 1995

With their permission, I'm sharing different faces of manipulation and control here, adding some of my own from my experiences with women:

Controlling Woman #1
Helpless Helen

Helpless Helen controls relationships by always being sick, needing help, always getting into trouble or always being sad. You are drawn to her because you feel guilty if you will not help her. Many times you really do want to help her. In Tagalog, these are the people who are *lampa* or accident-prone. Helen holds you in relationship by being such. Her life is always a tragedy. Without you, she dies. Fragility is the word to describe her strategy, and she puts up a front of helplessness in order to control you. The stance of Helen is: "Someone should always come through for me—and that's you. I require you to take hold of my world, so that I won't have to make decisions and I won't have to deal with relationships." Helen is never able to give. Instead, she hides behind weakness and never gives her heart to anyone.

Controlling Woman #2
Dummy Debbie

Dummy Debbie controls relationships by being dumb. Debbie is beautiful but looks naïve and fragile and acts like an airhead. Generally this has nothing to do with her IQ. She is really smart but she won't admit it. She would rather act dumb so that she would not be held responsible for the way she lives. Many times people go to Debbie and say, "*Ano ka ba, ang tanga-tanga mo!*" ("Why are you so dumb?"), to which she responds with a wide-eyed, "Huh? Why?" She's manipulatively helpless, and men are drawn to her because there's something sexual in her subtle girlishness. She has an aura of fragility that appeals to men and her coquettishness comes across seductively. She pretends she doesn't know her effect on men so that when men react to her with sexual innuendoes, she either drives them away or runs to another man to save her. Debbie would rather be dumb and act like she doesn't know much about relationships so that she can control people's expectations of her. In this way she can be absolved of any responsibility for what's going on in her life. When her relationships don't work, she can always fall back on, "I'm so sorry. I did not know."

Controlling Woman #3
Nicey Nina

Nicey Nina controls relationships by being nice. Actually, she is really nice! She is one lady I would always like to have around so I can use her! How evil of me! She is always pleasant, easygoing, kind and generous, supportive and warm. She's a people pleaser. She looks at satisfying all your needs, wants and desires. Nina wants to serve well with her hands but does not know how to give her heart to anyone. She avoids conflict with a passion. Her style of relating is to smother you with kindness. Nina says, "How can you be upset with me when I have been unbelievably good to you?" What she's really saying is, "I'm not required to relate to you. I'm giving you my service but not my heart." She serves people—to keep people out of her soul. In sex, Nina's husband feels like he's being serviced rather than desired.

Controlling Woman #4
Busy Bella

Busy Bella controls relationships by being busy. She's the "Busy Bee"—the administrator, the competent, thoughtful, reliable organizer. Bella combines the qualities of a nice girl who nevertheless is not afraid to say what's on her mind. Bella is hardly concerned with avoiding conflict. She is committed not to be vulnerable and will not stay long enough in a relationship to feel pain. She handles conflict by constantly being in motion and preoccupied with some kind of activity. Her basic style of relating is: "As long as I'm in action, I'm a hard target to hit." She can connect on an intellectual level but emotionally she can be stiff and cold. When you come into relationship with her, she keeps a certain distance. She tells you, "Stop right there, you have come far enough." Bella doesn't want to face the terror of being vulnerable with anyone.

Controlling Woman #5
Tough Terry

Tough Terry has a sign: "MEN, Keep out!" She controls her relationships by not letting you get near her and making you feel afraid of her. She has an edge that comes across as tough with sarcasm, cynicism and contempt. She says, "If you come to me and you fail me relationally, I have a way to make you pay." She enjoys outperforming men in male-dominated areas. Tough Terry presents this seductive challenge: "Go ahead and see if you can conquer me." In truth, Tough Terry wants to be conquered by the love of a genuinely strong man. But the risk of being hurt makes her quickly shift to being tough and competitive, eliminating any possibility of being relationally hurt again. She sets up hurdles for the man on the way to winning her heart, but the problem is, the obstacles she puts up looks something more like the 42k Psychological Marathon, the Relational Decathlon, and the Spiritual Grand Prix all rolled into one. What man can possibly win these? As a result, Tough Terry sets herself up for a double bind. The man loses, and so does she.

If Tough Terry continues to harden her heart, she can morph into...

Controlling Woman #6
Emasculating Emma.

This woman is the extreme version of Tough Terry. Having hardened her heart, she controls her relationships by defeating her man, rendering him weak and ineffective. She says, "If you want a relationship with me, then you must sacrifice your maleness. To whatever degree you are strong, I will weaken you and work toward your destruction." Destruction is centered on two areas—physical and emotional. These are the women who physically batter their men or abuse them verbally, or both. She has mastered the art of finding weakness in her man and exploiting it by highlighting his failures. She is terrified that if she discloses her heart to a man he can destroy her, so she would rather present an extremely tough façade and thus prevent herself from being hurt. She says, "If I let my heart be known to you, you can exploit my weaknesses and damage my heart." Therefore she is committed to not let her heart be known. Bottom line for Emasculating Emma is that she is never able to receive anything from her man.

Controlling Woman #7
Talkative Trisha

Talkative Trisha controls her relationships by talking incessantly. She is the life of the party. Conversations revolve around everything about her or what she thinks about other people. She needs to talk about something so that she doesn't have to let you into her life and see what's really going on in her heart. Silence terrifies her because she will be forced to listen to her soul and to other people. She cannot handle being vulnerable, and cannot tolerate quiet. Somewhere along the way, people avoid her often-shallow talk, and having to listen to her endless talking. But somehow she feels relieved that she does not have to be known. At home, she has trained her man to be quiet and brush him off. She pushes him into extra marital affairs and then she says, "See, its all your fault."

Controlling Woman #8
Sexy Sylvia

Sexy Sylvia manipulates and subjugates her man with the offer of her body. She relates to them with the promise of sex as long as she gets something in return. Social strategist and relationship guru Susan Walsh has this to say about women manipulating men with sex:

> Women still control the supply of sex. This is true in every culture and throughout time. Men have a strong desire for sex, and women control men's opportunities to get it... Traditionally, dating has been the way that men and women found common ground. It gives women a way to test out different men. Because women control the sex supply, men have sought ways to please women through romance. In the hookup culture, guys are receiving the message that girls are satisfied

> with hooking up, and have no expectations of them. In sending that message, girls forfeit the most powerful leverage they have over men: controlling the supply of sex. If girls demand love and kindness in return for sex, they will get it.[26]

If Sexy Sylvia is married, she withholds sex from her husband and makes him beg in return for sexual favors. She enjoys seeing her man having to beg for sex as this gives her power and control over him. Sex then becomes a reward for "good behavior" and good behavior is defined as giving Sexy Sylvia what she wants. Single Sexy Sylvia shows more cleavage and exposes more flesh because she wants to draw attention to herself. She wants to be admired for her body. After all the flirting and sex, Sexy Sylvia feels more frustrated because she knows that sex and seduction are cheap substitutes for what she really wants from her man.

Controlling Woman #9 Religious Ria

Religious Ria controls her relationships by being, looking and sounding very spiritual. All failures in relationships are the devil's fault and usually it's the attack of the devil on their lives. She uses this so that she doesn't have to take responsibility for her failures in relating to her man and sometimes even to the women in her life. At some point in her life, Religious Ria may have contemplated being a nun or a missionary but decided to get married. After having sex, Religious Ria feels very guilty. She tries to escape intimacy with her husband, leaving him very needy of her. Oftentimes she will hold him off in exchange for favors. She denies that her failures

[26] Susan Walsh, Sex: Men Desire It, and Women Control the Supply, (November 20, 2008), http://www.hookingupsmart.com/2008/11/20/hookinguprealities/sex-men-desire-it-and-women-control-the-supply. (Last Accessed: July 2010)

at relationship, the negative situations in her life, and her immature responses to hurts are her fault, nor will she admit that she has contributed to any of them. In the end she falls back into blaming that everything is the devil's fault: "The devil in me made me do it!" or "The devil in him made him do that to me!"

I know all these may sound like extreme descriptions of manipulative controlling women but it's not difficult to see that there's a grain of truth in each one. We probably can identify with one or two, or have been able to relate to some of them at some point in our lives. Whatever our verdict, they give us something to think about. It's good to reflect on how we as single women manipulate our world.

Lest you think this chapter is lopsided and against women, let me assure you that men manipulate and control too! Crabb has this to say:

> Unmanly men are controlling, destructive and selfish...When masculine energy is not released, when it is either suppressed or distorted, men:
>
> - Feel powerless; they compensate by committing themselves to control something. They become AGGRESSIVE MEN.
> - Experience rage and persuade them that vengeance is their due. They become ABUSIVE MEN.
> - Live with terror for which there is no resolution or escape, only relief. They dull the terror with physical pleasure and become ADDICTED MEN.[27]

So you see, men can resort to being just as controlling and manipulative in order to get what they want.

What Change Looked Like For Me

For my part, I am prone to control my world by being like Busy Brenda and Tough Terry. When I deal with men who have wounded my heart or when I see the possibility of being hurt by someone, sometimes I don't bother to find out if a man is good or not, I just leave. Or I become busy and I either flee or make things very hard for him. When a man has failed in his relationship with me, I make him

[27] Crabb, *Silence*, 47.

pay by not giving anything, much less my heart. That looks safer for me. Yet, when I do this, I know I miss out on welcoming good people into my life.

What does change from being a manipulative, controlling woman to being a vulnerable, God-pleasing woman look like for me? Actually, it's still a daily struggle. I must choose to daily rest my soul and trust God for things and people I cannot control. I must choose to allow myself to feel the pain of relationship and stay there and not run away from it. I must choose to put words to my pain and talk about it with God and with my friends instead of acting in anger or fear. In this way, I learn to be quicker to say, "When you did this, you hurt me…" I must then choose to go to the TRUE Lover of my soul to comfort my heart, listen to Him and allow Him to offer words that will soothe and heal my vulnerable female heart. I tell God about the men who hurt me and ask God to deal with them.

How successful am I? There are good days and bad days. Again, I am glad I can trust the Holy Spirit to live His life in and through me. When I walk in the power of the Spirit, it is easier to live in God's control and not mine. That is why it has to be a conscious effort on my part to rely on Him moment by moment and not on myself.

I believe it is possible to live with a soft, vulnerable, welcoming female heart and trust in the One who will protect and embrace me throughout my journey. Is there hope for a sinful woman like me? I believe so!

Journaling my Thoughts

★ What emotions were stirred in your heart as you read the different ways women can manipulate and control? Please write them down.

★ Who do you most identify with in the list of the controlling women?

★ How do you play out this form of control in your relationships with men and with other people?

★ When you are tempted to manipulate or become any one of the controlling women described, what are you trying to protect? What are you running away from?

★ When you realize the damaging impact of your control on other people, what do you feel?

★ Write your letter and your prayer to God here.

What Do You Do With Jerks?

CHAPTER TWELVE

12 What Do You Do With Jerks?

Aah, jerks! I had to google the word. One dictionary defines "jerk" as "a contemptibly obnoxious person." The urban dictionary has entries from apparently angry women who had quite a mouthful to say about jerks. One of them describes a jerk as "an insensitive, selfish, ignorant, cocky person who is inconsiderate and does stupid things."[28] Another describes a jerk as "the final stage of evolution of any male who spent at least one year dating in America, no matter his origin."[29] For the purposes of this chapter, we will define "jerk" as a mean, insensitive, heartless male who chooses to live only for himself. I will name him Jerky.

For The Love Of Starr

I had a beautiful six-year-old female golden retriever named Starr. Golden retrievers are known to be the most gentle, non-aggressive breed of dog. Starr had ehrlichiosis[30], which is a dengue fever-like disease that infects the canine species. At one time, Starr became very weak and dehydrated, and her platelet count went so low that she could have gone into a coma if she hadn't been treated. She also had pus and bloody discharges from her vulva, which must have been caused by

[28] http://www.urbandictionary.com/define.php?term=jerk, entry by "x8drea8x" (Last Accessed August 3, 2011)

[29] Urban dictionary, entry by "rafaleracer" (Last Accessed August 3, 2011)

[30] Ehrlichiosis is a bacterial disease transmitted by a certain type of brown ticks. Because the disease targets the white blood cells of dogs (much like dengue fever in human beings), if not treated quickly and properly, it may cause major internal bleeding, decreased immune responses, and eventually death.

pyometra, or an infection of her uterus. I called my vet friend, who told me to bring her in the morning for blood tests and other exams. Unfortunately, I had an 8 o'clock meeting with some officers of a company for a project we were doing. I decided I would bring Starr to my meeting first and then bring her to my vet friend. With my clinical eye, I could tell my dog was in a critical stage. Every movement was painful for her. But as I had to be in that meeting, I had to make the difficult decision to attend that meeting first and then bring Starr to the clinic. I knew that Starr could still make it provided I brought her to the vet's clinic around noon.

Early that morning, I parked in the garage of the office building and put Starr in the basement that had a few empty rooms and minimal movement of people. I could not leave her in the car because she might suffocate and destroy the door if she panicked. I figured the basement would be the best place for her since it would be cooler for her there. She would not be moving much because she was in pain and any movement would cause her more distress. I was confident that this was not going to pose any problem for people, since my dog had no aggressive bone in her system and at that time she was too weak to even notice people or move about. I asked a nurse in the adjoining room on the basement floor to keep an eye on her for me while I went to the meeting. I assured her that it would be a short one and I would be back soon. She agreed, seeing that Starr was very quiet and was still most of the time.

So off I went to my meeting.

Talk About Being Very Angry

Close to the end of the meeting, I got a note from the building secretary asking me to move my dog upon orders of the male administrator (who would be none other than Jerky). She said that Jerky had given instructions not to allow pets in the building. That surprised me. I had no idea about this policy because on more than two occasions I had seen a dog on one of the floors of the building. One of the employees had on occasion walked around and played with his pet dog in the lobby. At one time he even brought his dog to a meeting. What made him exempt from this "policy?"

I requested for just a few more minutes since my dog was sick and I intended to bring her to the vet right after the meeting.

To my horror, upon orders from Jerky, my sick dog had been forced to get up and walk 300 meters out of the basement through the adjacent car park and out of the building to a tin roofed shack beside a warehouse. For a dog that was ill and dehydrated, this was extremely stressful and difficult.

But like any golden retriever, Starr did not complain or whimper but followed obediently. When I went to look for her, I found her under the hot blistering sun—panting, confused and anxious. I was so afraid she would die. When I saw her, I cried in anger and dismay and lashed out at the lady who accompanied me. If this had happened in the US, I would have sued this man and the building owners, and I would have probably won in court.

I was not dumb to bring a dog that I knew would be aggressive and put human beings at risk. Couldn't Jerky have waited just a few more minutes until I finished my meeting so that I could bring her out myself? Or couldn't he have given me a fair warning before he bodily removed Starr from the basement?

I was told that Jerky had studied law but never passed the bar and so he ended up being an administrator of a building. I think that in his arrogance to prove he had power and authority over these small things, he went ahead so he would look big among his people.

I am sure you can sense my seething rage even as I write these words…ok…ok…calm down Orpah…calm down….

Jerky surfaced the issues in my heart

To make this story short, I was deeply hurt because Jerky was very insensitive to my situation. I responded in the only way I knew how, which was to react and retaliate in anger. I wonder how you would feel if you were torn between having to bring your sick dog to the hospital and having to stay for an important meeting, only to find out that an arrogant jerk had taken matters into his own hands and made your dog suffer in the process.

I wrote Jerky a letter that same night, even if I did not know him very well. But my mistake was that I wrote to him when I was still very angry and hurt. To spite him, I copy furnished his director and the Human Resources Head of the building. I asked him to apologize for each of my hurts and to suggest to me how he wanted to compensate me for the damages he caused my dog and me. What a mess I made just to have him pay! This was my angry, hurt heart wanting revenge. He did not reply to my email for a week. This silence made it worse for me. It felt like he brushed off my story as just another complaint from an unreasonable, hard-to-get-along-with woman.

Meanwhile I heard from others that Jerky was so distressed about my letter that he asked his leaders in the HR department what he should do. Later on, Jerky said he was sorry that he hurt me but he never acknowledged that what he did was wrong. He stuck to his policies.

When everything settled down, I realized I was so hurt and sad about the way Jerky responded to me and I to him. I was sad about my quick desire to hurt back when I was hurt, and about the way I wanted him to pay even to the point of emasculating him. I was sad because, honestly, I probably could have crushed his spirit even more. Yet by doing that I would have destroyed myself even more.

I was sad because it probably was not just Jerky *per se* but what Jerky represented that transported me back to the issues of my female heart not being handled well and not protected by men. As I look back at this story now, I ask myself, "After all you've learned about being soft and vulnerable, how would a feminine, non-manipulative, Spirit-filled, repentant, wonderful woman respond to jerks like these?"

Remember I told you that the very first emotion I learned was anger. Behind anger is deep pain. When I look back at this incident, what I have not told you yet was that the night before I brought Starr to the building en route to the vet, I was struggling in fear that I might lose her. Starr was my baby, and I was literally crying out to God to spare her. I was afraid that I had no control whether Starr would live or die. I was frustrated because although I was a veterinarian myself, I had neither means nor capacity to help my very own dog. Her condition was beyond me and so I had to ask for help from a vet friend. I was extremely anxious because

I knew it would cost money to have Starr treated, but as an act of faith I said I would simply go ahead and trust God.

I Wanted Something Else From Jerky

What was it that I really wanted Jerky to have done for me? I would have wanted him to be a little bit more sensitive. He could have bothered to find out why there was a dog in the basement in the first place. If he knew what I went through the night before then maybe he would not have done what he did. He would have known that my dog was in pain and that making Starr walk 300 meters in the heat would have possibly sent her on a heatstroke and into coma. I would have wanted him to be considerate, since I did not know about the No-Pets-Allowed policy and it would have been my first offense. I would have wanted him to tell me first, "Orpah, since we have a No-Pets-Allowed policy in this building, we cannot keep your dog in the basement. If it's all right with you, we will transfer your dog from this place to that place," to which I would have probably responded by jumping out of my meeting and moving Starr myself. That would have been more respectful of him.

This incident proved to me again that there would be people, some of them men, who would be incapable of handling my heart well and who would not treat me the way I wanted to be treated—and that would always be very painful. There will be men who will not come through for me. That's the sad fact, but a fact nonetheless.

I believe that NOT all men are like Jerky, though. There are good men who will have my good at heart, men who will genuinely want to know me, and help me meet my needs. There are men who will love me well, who will move courageously for my good. When they do come, I should be willing to welcome them and receive what they offer me.

It took me a long time to want to forgive Jerky, but I did. I wrote Jerky another letter saying that I had forgiven him.

The Jerkys who hurt me may or may not change. More often it will have to be my heart that will have to change. That's the truth I just need to wrestle with and grieve over.

I gave him another name: FJ—short for Forgiven Jerky.

Journaling my Thoughts

★ Who are the Jerkies in your life? How do you deal with them?

★ What did you really want these men to do for you as a woman?

★ How have you protected your heart from getting hurt?

★ Do you agree that not all men are jerks? What positive things do you know of men who are not jerks?

★ How would you welcome these real good, loving, authentic men who will want to do things for your good?

★ Write your letter and your prayer to God here.

Christmas, Valentine's Day, Weddings And A Funeral

CHAPTER THIRTEEN

13 Christmas, Valentine's Day, Weddings And A Funeral

What is it about Christmas, Valentine's Day, Thanksgiving, weddings and other occasions that make many of us single women depressed or very lonely? Every time I come away from events like these, I feel knotted up inside—and lonelier when I get home.

Urban legends and many articles in the USA show that major holidays like Christmas, Valentine's Day and Thanksgiving have the highest rates of suicides. I'm not sure if that's all accurate or if it's really just that, an urban legend. But I do know that if I did not know Jesus as my personal Savior and Lord and the True Lover of my soul, I could have easily been one of those statistics.

Thanksgiving in the US is always on the fourth Thursday of November. I know of a man who chooses to spend his birthday at an airport or on the road to another state every time his birthday happens to fall on Thanksgiving. I often wondered if he didn't have anyone to spend the special day with, and having it fall on Thanksgiving merely made it worse.

Holidays - Lonely Days

In my family, Christmases are among our most fun times. We usually start the celebration at my sister Leah's or my brother Lemuel's house. This is a time when the whole family has an excuse to eat pork, *crispy pata* (deep-fried pork knuckles), gallons of ice cream and other cholesterol-laden delights that are prohibited the rest of the year because they cause high blood pressure. But hey, Christmas is a once-a-year treat, so it's okay! It helps to have two medical doctors and a vet in the family, just in case…

It's also the time when all my nephews and nieces look forward to what they will find under the tree, which is usually t-shirts for the boys and nice blouses for the girls. After stuffing ourselves with food, it's time to open gifts, and it's usually my role to be the "elf" that distributes the gifts.

Afterwards, it's the tradition of our father *Tatay* to have all his nine grandchildren, line up in front of him and sing Christmas carols while he distributes very new, crisp bills of different denominations. This is the best part for everyone.

We sit and talk and eat again, sing some hymns, and then my *Nanay* will pray. In the afternoon, when it is time to go home, each one gathers up their stuff and their families and pack them all into their cars to go to their respective homes. I end up having to bring my parents back to their house.

Over the years, I have observed that every time we had to go, I would find myself getting angry or irritated at my parents, and I couldn't understand why.

Then it hit me. Behind anger is deep pain. I realized that it was too painful for me to face the time to go home, because each time I had to drive my parents and return to my empty apartment, it announced loudly what I did not have. It made more acute the longing in my heart to have a family of my own, a husband and children to go home to. Every year created a pattern of disappointment in my heart. Christmas pronounced this reality in my heart, and I needed to grieve over that.

Why Are Singles Not Remembered? Celebrated?

Then when February came, the whole cycle would repeat itself. I noticed that every time February came, I would always wish I were going away on a trip somewhere. A friend of mine who hates Valentine's Day makes it a point to wear black shirts out of spite for all those who wear red on that day.

Over the years, I have had so many disappointments about Valentine's Day. There was only one man who sincerely gave me a small card and said that I was his Valentine. It was sweet of him but then nothing came out of it.

In some churches, every Valentine's Day, couples are usually asked to stand up to be acknowledged. My former church has a tradition called the Cana Wedding, referring to the wedding that Jesus attended, that is celebrated or re-enacted twice a year, once on Valentine's Day and sometimes in June. Around this time also, many talks in churches center on what is popularly known as LCM, or love, courtship and marriage. The topics usually revolve around how married couples, or boyfriends and girlfriends, should treat each other.

Why are there no Valentine Sundays that celebrate singleness or celebrate the gifts that singles offer to the church? Why are we not celebrating older singles, these lovely people who have ministered to countless men and women and blessed them out of their singleness? Unfortunately, every time there are celebrations like these in the church, the singles are left out.

In silence, I scream, *"Hey, what about us?!"* Somehow, many churches tend to isolate, alienate, or simply neglect singles.

An ex-single male friend of mine in Seattle describes a classic example of the way churches deal with those who are not married and have no children. Let me allow Dean to tell his own story:

> *Here is my funny but sad story about when I was new to this area, still single, and was looking for a home church. I visited one church and the pastor wanted to drive home the point that the message he was about to deliver was for EVERYONE, so he said, "All the children repeat after me, 'This sermon is for me.' All the teenagers repeat after me, 'This sermon is for me.' All the parents repeat after me, 'This sermon is for me.' All the grandparents repeat after me, 'This sermon is for me.' He was perfectly confident that he had included everyone, but he left me out. (He counted the grandparents twice.) I'm sure he was totally unaware of his blunder. I wondered if anyone else noticed. The church seemed to be so completely family-oriented*

that they may not have known there was any such thing as a person over the age of 20 with no kids. He went straight from teenagers to parents—wow! Obviously I was not going to fit in. (The message was not for me.) I was over 40 and had yet to produce a single offspring. What a freak! Needless to say, I never went back. By the way, his incredibly important message that he wanted to make sure no one missed was about...uhm... something really important, I'm sure.

All I am saying is, it is hard to live as a single person in a world that focuses on and ministers to married people and their families.

How does one deal with the loneliness that creeps in on special occasions like this? There are so many ways men and women try to fill this loneliness. For me, ice cream always works! Or I just chill out the whole afternoon and watch Korean *telenovelas*. By the time I finish my ice cream and my eyes are sore and bulging from watching too many *telenovelas*, I end up more depressed.

I believe there is a better way. There has got to be a better way to deal with these momentary light afflictions!

Where To Take Our Disappointments

I've been encouraged by good mentors in my life to take all my disappointments to God. But what does that look like? First of all, it took me two arduous years of facing the truth about myself through my Biblical Counseling course. The years after that then led me on a journey where I came to realize that taking my disappointment to God means learning to go to God instead of turning to cheap substitutes for God like shopping, raiding the fridge, or busying myself with work. I have found that going to God means learning to entrust my soul completely to Him, conversing with Him or groaning before Him about the pain of being alone. In times like these, I cry when I have to. I allow myself to feel and embrace the pain of not having what I want. This is in contrast to my old protective stance of convincing myself, "It's ok, I can do this alone. I don't need other people! I won't allow myself to feel the pain now because I won't be able to handle that. I will numb the pain by drowning myself in what will satisfy me NOW!"

Going to God may mean painstakingly opening the Word of God even when I don't want to, in the hope that God will speak good words to my soul. After settling my heart with God, then I can go talk about it to my girlfriend or have dinner with friends. Or then maybe later I may cry some more.

Idolatry Defined

George Blake once said that:

> An idol is anything that we go to first, instead of God, to avoid being vulnerable or to diminish the pain of uncomfortable realities.[31]

The uncomfortable painful reality is that, no man really wants my heart right now. To avoid this pain I drown myself in illusory things. I go to girlfriends who may comfort me by telling me, "Those jerks are missing out on you, Orpah." Or I go to food to give me quick fullness of stomach, or to love stories on TV that give me the illusory hope that maybe someone will pursue me the way they do on TV. The last thing I do is go to God.

I think that for us women, our idols are food, shopping, work, busyness, romance books, *telenovelas*, email, Facebook, drinking, and so forth. For men, idols may mean being distant from relationships, putting in excessive time at work or *barkada*[32] nights, drowning themselves in sports, drinking, gambling, substance abuse, and pornography.

To whom then should my heart and my eyes look as the source of my life? Exodus 6:2 says, "God spoke further to Moses and said to him, *I am the LORD.*" God IS! What an amazing revelation from God about who He is when he revealed himself to us as the great I AM. He gave us a promise that He will be an ever-present reality to His people. Now I know that God through Jesus Christ is the only source of my life, and I am glad He is the one who pursues me and doesn't give up making me see this truth.

---

[31] Blake, lecture notes

[32] *Barkada* is a Filipino term for a group of friends who love to hang out together.

When I was about to turn 50, it hit me that I had no house, no family, and no children who would pass on my good genes. I had no man to kiss me goodnight and sleep with. No man to wake up and make breakfast for (this one I didn't mind at all!).

Sometimes, a single woman like me has to face disease, like cancer. By God's grace I don't have cancer. I have asked God to please arrange my death not through that route but to simply let death come to me while I'm sleeping so that I'll wake up in heaven. Is that possible? Why not? I believe God will honor our hearts' desire, even in the manner of our death.

It is New Year 's Eve as I write this chapter. I have decided to stay on top of a mountain at a house owned by my cousin. I came up here with my dog, Starr. I wonder if anyone misses me.

Grieving The Person I Wanted To Become

At this point, I grieve at the many losses at this stage of my life. I learned from Dr. Philip Ney that for a person to better accept who she is at present, she first needs to grieve the death of the person she wanted to become.

The person I envisioned myself to become is a married woman with four kids—a wife helping her husband to grow and develop into the man God wants him to be—in short, a helpmeet for him. Everyone would be proud of my husband and he would be a happy man. We would be traveling, singing, and together making wonderful music for Jesus. People would be worshipping God through our lives. We would be helping people with broken hearts and lives to find healing in Jesus.

That's the person I wanted to become but will never be. Not anymore.

The reality is, I am now in my pre-menopausal stage and I cannot have four children anymore. At this point, no man is pursuing my heart. I have not sung for a long time. I can still sing praises to God and usher people into worship but I'll be doing that without a husband. I will still be helping people with broken lives find Jesus, but—yes, you guessed it—I will be doing that as a single woman. This may all sound morbid to you, but you see, I need to grieve over these things and accept the truth that, yes, I will never be that happily married woman anymore.

And when I have accepted this, then I can better embrace and accept who I am now. I do not need to get angry and clench my fist at God and demand, "God, you owe me!" The truth is, He does not owe me anything. I owe Him a life lived well, married or not.

As Christians, we are taught to rejoice in the Lord always. But in some Christian circles, this beautiful command has been distorted to mean that we must deny the reality of loss or the necessity of grief in our lives. But when understood properly, grief is good. Grief is healthy. If we do not grieve well, it becomes a pathologic grief that turns into depression.

Grieving Over The Little Deaths

A great explanation about grief was given by Nancy Groom from her book *Heart To Heart About Men*. This is what she says:

> God calls us to be honest with Him about what is in our hearts—even our anger about the unfairness of what has happened to us as a result of living in a fallen world. We may not be as blatantly uninhibited as that little girl in her tantrum. After all, we as adult women have devised sophisticated ways to hide or redirect our rage so that we'll look good, even to our selves. But the rage is there and like the screaming child, we cannot be held by the One who loves us unless we are willing to move beyond the tantrum into heartbreak and from the heartbreak into partaking of His own sweet grace, which deeply satisfies. Our hearts long for tenderness and rest, but raging children cannot be comforted until they cry. Then their tears can be wiped away, and they can rest and be kissed while they sleep...When we are driven to Him and lay down our rage, then we enter sorrow and grief and can rest in His kind arms.[33]

So how then do I deal with the truth that Christmas, Valentine's Day and many other celebrations will continue to come my way to remind me that I don't have what I long for? I will need to grieve well over those little deaths. Death to what I should have had, death to

---

[33] Nancy Groom, *Heart to Heart About Men* (Colorado Springs, CO: Navpress,1995), 99.

what I should have become. I will grieve, but will still walk with people with a heart that is alive, in contrast to a hard, angry, impenetrable heart. I will set up a symbolic funeral and a burial of all these deaths so I can live again with a different heart.

I want to be able to give my soul for the good of another. I want to be able to trust people enough to receive what they offer me and hope that in turn they will respect this trust and handle my heart well. But whether or not they will, I want to continue living with a good, open and welcoming heart.

This is a very hard thing for me to do. It means a daily commitment to live this way.

You ask: tell me again why we need to do this? We need to be able to acknowledge our disappointments before God and grieve over the losses in our lives before we can receive the comfort that God offers. When we experience God's comfort, then Jesus becomes real to us. The reality of His presence gives rest to our souls and enables us to live according to God's design for us as women who are not afraid to be soft and vulnerable, are able to grieve well and truly rejoice in who we are, and who live with courageous and valiant faith.

So Christmas? Valentine's Day? Weddings? Bring them on!!!

Journaling my Thoughts

★ Do Christmases, Valentine's Days and weddings affect you? If so, how?

★ What do you do and where do you go so as not to feel the pain of disappointment in your life?

★ How do these quick fixes become idols in your heart?

★ What do you understand about grief? Have you welcomed grief in your life? How?

★ What would your life look like today if everything that you had wanted to happen in your life did happen? Describe this picture.

★ Which parts of this picture do you need to grieve over and bury?

★ Take time to grieve. Write down what it means for you to go back to the Lover of your soul and bring to Him all your disappointments.

★ Write your prayer to God here.

Why Aren't You Married Yet?

CHAPTER FOURTEEN

I'M SINGLE,
NOT BROKEN.

14 Why Aren't You Married Yet?

Painful Questions, Painful Answers

I have mastered the art of giving pat answers to these questions:

WHY aren't you MARRIED yet?

Mahirap magpakasal mag-isa, magastos!

(It's hard to get married alone—it's expensive!)

WHY aren't you MARRIED yet?

Bukas na lang, tanghali na kasi eh!

(Maybe tomorrow, it's lunchtime now…)

WHY aren't you MARRIED yet?

Because my boyfriend ran off with my ex-boyfriend…

At the airport in Penang, Malaysia, on my way to Bangkok one November, I read from a newspaper: "Woman says 'I do' to self!" I thought that must be the most pathetic thing any woman could do.

I don't look forward to weddings or clan reunions because I usually have to put up a hard exterior against seemingly good-hearted men, women, and married couples who ask me why I'm not married yet. In my brain I say to them, *"Oh, come on! Can't you see that if I had the chance I would have gotten married yesterday?*

Why aren't you married yet? These words make me feel like it's all my fault for remaining unmarried until now. How do you want us singles to answer that question? If I told you, *"Nobody wants me. That's why I'm not married yet,"* would that suffice?

I realize that there's just nothing people will say about my being single that will comfort my soul.

When people say, *"Don't worry, Orpah, you'll find a man soon,"* I think, *"Oh really? When? Where? Why not now?"*

Or when people say, *"Oh well, it's his loss that he didn't pursue you!"* I think, *"Why does he have to lose? Can't we both win?"*

Or the more charismatic ones say, *"In Jesus' name, you will get married this year."* That was 1998.

How Not To Handle Singles

In general, the community of believers does not really know how to deal with its singles. Well-meaning believers tend to see us as a disease that has no actual cure, so they treat the secondary infection instead. They deal with us like we are hovering spirits and if they are tenacious enough to deal with other stuff, these bad spirits will simply disappear. We are like boils that need to be injected with a strong antibiotic, and if given the proper medicine, we might end up being healed!

One of the most hilarious times I had in dealing with singleness was when my father visited me in our house at the Campus Crusade for Christ single women's apartment. After having lunch and talking with us for a while, in all his love and honesty, he asked, "So you are all unmarried women here in this house?" I said "Yes, Pops," after which he then went on to pray that we would all get married sometime. He even went on to declare, *"And in Jesus' name, I command the spirit of singleness to COME OUT!"* And we acted like we all fell into a trance and tumbled backwards, as though the so-called spirit of singleness had just come out of our stomachs. We all came out laughing with my father! Oh my *Tatay*! Bless his heart! Well, it's not a bad idea to drive away the spirit of singleness if it's a curse or a bad spirit, right?

Which drives me to my point. Good-hearted individuals—friends of ours, and church mates—sometimes don't know how to nourish our souls as single individuals.

There is a man I truly love as my older brother, but sometimes he hurts me without his knowing it. Larry now and then teases me about another male friend who happens to be single. Today, that single male friend doesn't want to have anything to do with me. He knows that his friendship with me becomes a springboard for Larry's teasing. He hates being set up so he backs off, and we both miss out on the joys of friendship.

Sometimes my friend says things like, "Okay Orpah, you need to lose weight now so he'll like you." Or after introducing me to a so-called prospect, he says, "Orpah, what happened? Why didn't he court you?" as if it were my fault that this man didn't so much as look at me!

An older lady friend of mine told me that maybe I did not know how to flirt! Another man who rode in my car remarked that it was no wonder I didn't have a husband—I drove a black car and had a horse ornament hanging from my rearview mirror! Because of that, "no one would be crazy enough to court me," he said. If I had an eject button in my car, I would have ejected that man right there and then.

I try my very best to understand these good-hearted people. First of all, based on the premise that I know they love me and all other singles in our organization, I have come up with a few hypotheses. I always hear them say, "These single ladies are the smartest, the best-trained individuals, they do great ministry and are also very beautiful—why aren't they married? Something needs to be done!"

Maybe they're alarmed at the increasing statistics of single, unmarried women, and so feel they have to do something. Or maybe they're thinking of the future to the extent that they feel they need to propagate the line of godly women married to godly men up to the fourth generation. Or maybe they feel that single men are not exerting enough to meet more of these ladies, and so need to give them a little push so that something wonderful would happen.

Couples who got married at ages 45 and above seem to have this all-out war to battle singleness just because they believe that if they managed to get married at that age, then we singles all should be able to do the same thing too. I believe they sincerely want us to experience the ups and downs of wedded bliss, but in their desire to do that, all they see is that we singles need "fixing." Their guess is that something's wrong with our social lives—we singles are not out there enough, we are in our holes, we don't go out on dates. So they sponsor dates in restaurants, they pay a whole year of Christian singles website membership, and the only thing they have not done is to have a Singles Conference only for single men and women age 45 and above.

These are all great efforts and we love them for what they do. For those who successfully found their partners as a result of these ministrations—halleluYAH! But what about those singles who, despite their best attempts, still found that things didn't work out?

It creates tension in our soul because when expectations fall short, it almost always looks like it's our fault. Even with their best intentions at heart, somewhere along the way, all these movements exhaust us and set us up for more disappointments.

If You Want To Bless Single Women...

So what should these well-meaning brothers and sisters do?

I don't know. It's not for me to tell them to stop what they're doing because I understand their good intentions. But maybe they should do things with more caution and greater sensitivity. Careless comments and attitudes hurt us more than many can imagine. It's easy to find all sorts of reasons to say, *"That's why you don't have a husband."*

At this point I just want to say that I believe not all women are called by God to be married. Some women are called to be single. In fact some women embrace singleness and feel fulfilled in living out God's calling for them to be single. They feel their purpose in life is best lived out as a single woman. One lady missionary has purposely said, "Some women will have to remain single, to some this was a given. I was one of those specially hand picked by God to remain single. This was part of my discipleship. Others were to grow in the Lord in the context of marriage, mine was in the context of singleness...Once I saw the magnitude of His kingdom work, many issues, including my singleness, became secondary."

Let me switch quickly and include married couples as my audience now. This is going to be more like a plea or a cry for help. Married men and women need to welcome us single people just as we are. I assure you we are not sick. We have no disease just because we are single. I believe we need married couples to minister to us as single men and women. We need you to love us well, and not do more damage to our hurt souls. We don't need you to pronounce the obvious, or manage us to make us become like you.

Invite Us In

There are many ways you can minister to us as single individuals. One of the most important is simply to invite us in. Invite us to enter your world just as we are, with no expectations. We need you to welcome us just as we are—single people who are not compelled to get married.

We need you to welcome us with our unmet longings and allow us to be. Welcome our uniqueness. Find out what we like and what we are good at and see us blossom from there.

It used to be that American Campus Crusade for Christ missionary couples invited us single people into their homes for dinner, for babysitting, to concerts, or just to have fun in their home. I have not experienced that since my friends John and Sandy Mackin, and Fel and Lorie Yturralde went back home to the US.

Invite us to have dinners with you. It can be an informal or a special dinner. It will help us if you ask us about how we are doing in our personal life, and not just about work. Be authentic in wanting to minister to us. Ask questions that will help us talk and not be defensive about our status as single people.

Valentine's Days are difficult for us but you can include us in your celebrations of love and friendship. Couples can give flowers to the single ladies on Valentines Day, and that will speak to us a lot. Don't do it in an organized every-single-lady-gets-one-flower kind of style. It would be nice if you really thought of us individually. If you didn't think of us, it would still be ok. You wouldn't want to fake it and neither would we. As a person or a household, you may host a Valentine's Day dinner as a fun party and not for the purpose of setting us up for a date. A clean fun night would be enough for us.

In churches, you can devote one Valentine's Day weekend to talk about singleness in the pulpit, and celebrate singleness. Then you can ask us how you can pray and minister to us.

One fun thing that my organization leaders and I did last Sadie Hawkins' day (Leap year day, or February 29, which comes every four years) was to treat all the single ladies to a very nice dinner in a fine dining restaurant. We asked them to dress up and we just let them eat, laugh, and have fun. We treated them to good live music from a famous lady singer as she dedicated all her songs to these ladies. Our friends went away full in their hearts, welcomed as they were and ready to live life again as single women.

I think I mentioned in a previous chapter one good thing that a married man did for my soul on Valentine's Day. I was then grieving over another man who had promised he would come to see me on that day but for some reason, he did not. I was devastated. But on V-day, I woke up to a vase of beautiful flowers and a card that said, "Valentine's is not just for couples and girlfriends but for special friends like you!" It was from my married friend. He had a nicer, bigger vase for his wife of course.

Having said all these, let me add that the posture of our hearts as singles will be that we do hope for the best but we may expect the worst. This means that our hope is not dependent on whether or not people will minister to us during these difficult times. We know that there will be times when people will forget us, and times when people will not love us the way we want to be loved or ministered to. This doesn't mean we have to respond in anger or self-pity, but we can choose to accept our circumstances graciously and joyfully receive what life and friends have to offer us. We can invite ourselves to your homes, right? Or we can create our own wholesome parties, too.

Needed: Prayers

More than anything, what would minister to us is if you will pray for us. Pray that we will continue to live with a heart that's alive and real. Pray for us that in our loneliness, we will not run to other gods but instead will draw closer to the one True Lover of our souls, and allow Him to fill us! Pray that we can keep ourselves pure until Jesus comes back.

Even as we struggle, we will receive whatever will be offered to our souls and we will enjoy sweet fellowship and love from you. We will want to offer the warmth that comes from our hearts so you can also enjoy us and learn from us. You might be surprised that there's a lot to learn from many of us!

As a single person, I know I need to manage my heart in a way that, whether or not there are people who care for me, I can take care of my soul and my body. It will be wrong of me to demand from you, or from married couples, to fill our souls. I have no illusion that you can do that.

So I am looking forward to being welcomed by you into your life and your family and your home. Please don't give up on us. Not just yet.

SO if anyone is going to ask me this question again today, why aren't you married yet? I'll say,

"Ask God!"

Journaling my Thoughts

- ★ What are the usual reactions you get when people learn that you are still single?

- ★ What are some hurtful words that many people have jokingly said about your being single? Why do these words hurt? What would you want to tell them in response?

- ★ If you're a single person, in what ways can you invite people into your life so that they can discover and enjoy you more? Take out your planner, IPAD, cell phone or laptop calendar so you can list action points and schedule when this will happen.

- ★ How can you reach out to both singles and married couples in order to bless them? List action points and schedule when this will happen.

★ Write your letter and prayer to God here.

Of Starrs and Chloes

CHAPTER FIFTEEN

15 Of Starrs And Chloes

I know many single people from all over the world who would rather own a dog than be married to a man. I love my dogs! But If I had a choice, I'd still want a husband! Really!

A famous veterinarian, Dr. James Herriot, wrote the book *All Creatures Great and Small,* which I read when I was a teenager. He related the awesome adventures of working with God's creatures. Like Dr. Herriot, I find God is beautiful in this way. I worship God in His creation. I love seeing foals, puppies, even goats when they are born. They are such beautiful, majestic works of God. In the mountain in Canada I enjoyed various species of birds and the huge dogs. I also enjoyed the stinky seals when we sailed out to sea.

During my growing up years, I've always had at least one dog. I couldn't imagine living life without them. In fact, I loved dogs so much that I remember my father in one of his bad moods spanking me as a little girl because I would kiss the dog but would not kiss him! My defense was, "But my dog has whiskers and you don't!"

The Risk Of Loving

If it were my commitment to be safe or not to get hurt in relationships with men, then I would do what C.S. Lewis warned about in his book *The Four Loves:*

> There is no safe investment. To love at all is to be vulnerable. Love anything, and your heart will certainly be wrung and possibly broken. If you want to make sure of keeping it intact, you must give

> your heart to no one, not even to an animal. Wrap it carefully round with hobbies and little luxuries; avoid all entanglements; lock it up safe in the casket or coffin of your selfishness. But in that casket—safe, dark, motionless, airless—it will change. It will not be broken; it will become unbreakable, impenetrable, irredeemable. The alternative to tragedy or at least to the risk of tragedy is damnation. The only place outside heaven where you can be perfectly safe from all the dangers and perturbations of love is Hell.[34]

You know, I would rather have a heart that is alive and vulnerable than a heart that is safe, dark, impenetrable and lifeless. And it's true—if I love or keep a dog for a pet, it would deeply hurt me if it died. Does that mean that I should not get one at all? No way! Dogs oftentimes fill a hole in our lives as single people as they meet our need to take care of someone. Because we don't have children, we can always take care of a dog. But of course we won't mind babysitting your kids…okay, maybe just once in a while.

For the past five years, I have learned many beautiful lessons about God and my relationship with Him through Starr, my seven-year old Golden Retriever, and Chloe, my six-year old Jack Russell Terrier. They are wonderful, loyal, loving hairy companions. But delightful as they are, and even though they are wonderful creatures, they do not come close to having a husband! And they will never be able to take away my pain of being single.

Busy Chloe: Hides From Her Master

Chloe is my smart, hyperkinetic, sweet, schizophrenic Jack Russell. She is one dog with an attitude! She acts as the queen of my house. She has a mind of her own. So many times, even against my will she would do stuff that she knows would get her into trouble with me. Despite her training to pee only in places that she was trained to, she would pee in the off-limits spots, especially when I would be out the whole day. Afterwards she runs off and hides from me. She expects me to run after her though, and deal with her accordingly.

---

[34] C.S Lewis, *The Inspirational Writings of C.S. Lewis* (New York, NY: Inspirational Press, 1960), 278-279.

There are days when I'd come home and immediately I would know that Chloe had done something she was not supposed to do. I would know this because she would have this guilty Chloe look. I would ask her, "Chloe, what did you do?" And she would have this pitiful, really remorseful look on her face, with her docked tail behind her legs, as she led me to the crime scene. After which I would talk to her and explain that she needed to be disciplined because of what she had done.

Now this is what is so interesting about Chloe. Right after the discipline, Chloe quickly switches to a posture of relief and she is now all over me, loving and kissing me and acting like nothing happened. Chloe immediately knows she is forgiven and she has paid for her crime. Now her heart is at rest and she can continue to love and fellowship with me. This makes me ask myself, "What am I hiding from my Master that causes me not to enjoy my fellowship with Him?"

My heart is amazed at how this becomes a picture of God and me. Many times He welcomes my sincere desire to say "I'm sorry" and as soon as I acknowledge my wrong and I receive His forgiveness, immediately the barrier that separates me from Him and that which keeps me from fellowshipping with Him melts away. I can climb onto His lap, love Him and let Him love me.

On regular days, I come home expecting Chloe to come rushing to greet me. However, there are days when, even if I strain to call her and command her to come, Chloe would not come to me or even look at me because she would be too busy trying to catch the mouse under the washing machine. She would not stop until she had caught the poor rodent and that would be the only time she'd notice that I was home. In Chloe's busyness with something, she can't enjoy me and I can't enjoy her too. I often need to think, what are some of the things I do independently of God that causes me not to enjoy God as I should?

Loyal Starr: Desires To Please Her Master

Between Chloe and Starr, I would rather be like Starr who gives me a picture of how I should be in my relationship with God. Golden retrievers were designed by God to have no aggressive bone in their system. They are highly sociable animals. They are gentle, loving creatures. Starr's desire is simple, and that is to please me, her Master. She wants to have constant contact with me. She wants to be where I am. If she doesn't see me, she gets lonely.

When I bring her to a gathering, her eyes are fixed on me. Everyone may call her name or get excited about her but her eyes would be where I am, and if at any time I am not within her view, she will go look for me. There may be noise all around her and people calling her, but she responds only to my call. She knows my voice from afar.

Without me in the house, she becomes uneasy and sad. When I am out, my roommates wonder why Starr mopes the whole day. Then at the sound of my car, her whole countenance quickly changes. Her ears prop up; she stands at attention and looks out of the window until I come in.

She then has this satisfied growl as she welcomes me with her teddy bear toy in her mouth. When she welcomes me, she wiggles her tail and sways her hips in what I would call her welcome dance! It's actually beautiful to behold, and as her master, I watch her with joy and love.

Do I Have A Chloe Heart Or A Starr Heart?

Everyday, I compare myself to Starr. Am I as excited to meet with Jesus? More often, I am not. I am more eager to open my computer and see what email I got during the night or find out what's going on in Facebook. This makes me think, what do I have to offer or give to Jesus when I welcome Him each day? How do I live out my life in a way that will honor Him? How do I make Jesus smile? Is it finally sharing Christ with an officemate in spite of my busyness? Or is it just the victory of keeping my integrity--in my thought life, in paying taxes, or in just having the strength to say No?

Starr is a dog after my own heart. Starr senses the condition of my heart when I am grieving or when I am angry or am just simply at rest. One time I felt so sad over something that I just needed to cry. I was on my bed and Starr came to see and check out my face. When she saw I was crying, she stayed right there in front of me and let me cry my heart out to her.

Starr quickly senses my mood. When she does something that angers me, like when she destroys some plants she digs in the garden, she would lovingly and courageously come to me, with her mouth and her feet still full of dirt, in sincere repentance knowing that what she did was wrong. Unlike Chloe who would hide and deny her wrongdoing, Starr does not run off. As Starr's master, I cannot keep my anger long.

Starr knows how to express her need. When she needs to go out and do her thing in the middle of the night, she pokes her face into my face or makes a loud whimper. If that doesn't work, another poke of her toy in my face would be enough to wake me.

There are days when Starr would get very scared of loud sounds, especially when she happens to be out of the house. Because she's a very big and strong dog, she would destroy anything—doors, screens, metal handles—just so she could get inside. She quickly runs to me when she is afraid and I welcome her to hide under my bed or at least embrace her to reassure her it's okay. She unashamedly tells me when she wants things, and as her master, for as long as I am able to give it, I do my best to give her what she wants.

Do I courageously come to Jesus despite any sin I may have done, and quickly repent of it? Do I abhor sin the way Jesus does? Do I know the forgiving heart of my Master well enough to be able to trust Him and jump onto His lap and rest? Am I open enough to tell God my need and am I willing to express my need clearly and patiently wait for His answers?

WHY IS THERE A MAN AND HE'S NOT MINE? Starr and Chloe remind me of how I should be with my Sweet Jesus whether I have a husband or not. My desire should be simple: to please Him as I walk with Him and to always be by His side. Starr and Chloe have taught me that:

I should be sensitive to God's heart and be intimate with Him. I should know what grieves Him and what gives Him joy.

When Jesus calls, I should respond even amid the noise and circumstances around me. He is the only one whom I should listen and respond to.

I should be willing to welcome Jesus with something that I can offer to Him.

I can come to Him in repentance and not run away when I make mistakes. Even if I have grieved His heart, I am assured that He will welcome my repentance and will forgive me.

I can freely come to Jesus with my needs knowing that I can "poke" Him and be relentless in my asking. If He sees it's good for me, I can rest in the truth that He will give it to me because I know He is a good Master. When He doesn't give what I ask, it will still be for my own good.

I want my life—who I am and who I am becoming--to give joy to my Master. I want to offer to Him the gift that is my life!

Journaling my Thoughts

★ Are you a Starr or a Chloe? Why do you say so?

★ Have you made similar observations about God's creation that give you insight about God's character, our relationship with God, and God's dealings with us?

★ In what ways can you be more responsive towards God in ways that will please Him?

★ Write your prayer to God here.

Have Visa, Will Travel!

CHAPTER SIXTEEN

16 Have Visa, Will Travel

Who says that if you are single, life will be boring? Well, my single life has been anything BUT boring. One of my annual joys is trusting God for big things, and that involves traveling.

In 1997, a girlfriend, Chantal, gave me a leather passport holder and said, *"Here, Orpah, travel the world!"* Little did she know the impact those words would have on my life. Since then, I have been traveling the world. The only continents I haven't been to, but would like to visit, are Latin America and Antarctica. (Hint! Hint! To my friends there...yoo-hoo?) Some of you may say, "Big deal!" Well it IS a big deal for me—a single missionary lady! How is someone like me able to travel the world?

As I am writing this chapter, I am in the home of my good friends Rey and Angie Luciano in Sydney, Australia. I promised I would mention them for being my gracious, loving hosts as I wrote the first few chapters of this book! Australia would be the 30th country that I have visited in the past 15 years.

Miracle Prayer List

Years ago, I read from the book, *The Prayer of Jabez* by Bruce Wilkinson, about a person who made a miracle prayer list. I adopted that concept and started making my own list that same year. At each birthday and New Year's Day, I would look back at how God has answered my prayers, and then I would update and add to that list.

When my birthday comes, first on my agenda for the day is an unhurried, sweet breakfast date with the Special Man in my life, Jesus

Christ! I go to my favorite restaurant in Quezon City, which serves wonderful breakfast and has a very romantic ambience. On those morning dates I write down everything from the past year that I want to thank God for, including my family, my work, and my ministry accomplishments. I then say, "*Thank you, God. Thank you for the fun I had. Thank you that I am still single, as You want me to be today. Thank you that I am not a disgruntled, miserable single old woman who misses out on the joys of life just because she's single. Thank you for my wrinkles, for according to the concert artist, Sandi Patty, 'Wrinkles don't hurt!'*"

When I made my first miracle prayer list, it included four different things. At that time, I was a single missionary with no property, no bank account to show, and it was financially impossible for me to go anywhere in North America. Unfortunately, this is the reality of living in a third world country like the Philippines. Every time we go on a trip, we need to get a visa, except when we're traveling to Israel and anywhere within Southeast Asia. Because the Philippines is a member of the Association of South East Asian Nation Treaty (ASEAN), we Filipinos enjoy travel privileges to other ASEAN countries. Israel, on the other hand, allows us to go to their country without a visa because, during the Diaspora, we were the only Asian country that welcomed Jews to our shores. Ours was also one of the last decisive votes needed in the United Nations that paved the way for Israel to be recognized as a country. So we love Israel and Israel loves us!

My First Miracle Prayer Request: USA And Canada Trip

My first miracle prayer request went like this: "*God, I would like to go on an all-expense-paid, round-trip tour to the United States of America and I don't want to raise finances for this. I would like it to be a wonderful surprise gift from someone. I don't know how You'll do that, but thank You in advance for the answer to this prayer!*"

Two years later, this is exactly what happened. One day, an American couple who are dear friends of mine and had no idea that I prayed this prayer, called me up out of the blue. They said, "Hey

Orpah, we miss you so much, we would like you to come to the States and see us. Plot out your itinerary and we will pay for your whole trip!" I said, "Whaaah?!" It turned out that a grandmother of theirs had passed away and had left them some money. They said God had told them to call me and give me this all-expense-paid trip to the USA! I praised God that this couple listened to God's voice and responded. God used their grandmother to be the answer to the first of my many, many miracle prayer requests! HalleluYAH!

The next part of that first miracle was how I got my visa to the USA. During the 80's and 90's in the Philippines, because of our economy, there had been a growing number of people who traveled to the US but never came back. They stayed in the US illegally until they got a legitimate job offered by a legitimate company that was willing to sponsor them.

At that time, I had all the makings of a person who might never come back to Manila. I was a single female, I had no good bank records to prove any wealth, and I had neither records of properties to hold me to my country nor a high-paying job that would guarantee that I would come back to Manila. Everything should have alarmed them that I could easily be one of those who could be an illegal migrant or an illegally overstaying tourist.

But miraculously, the consul did give me a visa! Despite all odds, God answered this first miracle prayer request of mine. This US visa was key to many of my other trips outside the country. During that time you could not be given a visa to enter Canada or any part of Europe unless you had a US visa.

That first US trip was more than wonderful! I visited friends in Minneapolis-St Paul, Minnesota, Indiana, Illinois and California. Then I went to New York to particularly meet up with a Christian artist, Makoto Fujimura. I met Mako when he was in Manila in the 90's and as he observed the ministry I had with the artists, he caught a vision to start his own artist's ministry in New York. I was so encouraged that Mako was able to start the artist's ministry called the International Artists Movement (IAM). As a result of Mako's ministry, many other artists in New York heard about God's love and forgiveness and he encouraged them to express their newfound faith through their art. Today, he has left that ministry to his disciples and has continued this ministry back in Japan.

Mako, as my NY host, encouraged me to watch *Les Miserables*—my first Broadway show. I watched it all by myself! My favorite musical ever! I must be sick in the head to love New York as many say, but I really do love New York, because I'm an artist at heart and I love the mixture of art, culture, the bustle of the city and the craziness of the place.

That was the first of many trips that opened a whole new world of looking at life and discovering different and amazing people in all my travels.

Let me give you a classic example. A few years after Chantal gave me the leather passport holder, she called and excitedly asked, *"Orpah, how would you like to go to Canada?"* At that time, because I had a friend in LA whom I wanted to see, I said, "Sure!" not even knowing what the trip was about. Then I asked, "So why am I going to Canada again?" Chantal then explained that God brought my name to her mind when she was thinking of someone to take her place in the Hope Alive Group counseling training to be held in Victoria, Canada the following month.

Hope Alive is a group counseling ministry that helps stop the epidemic of abuse, neglect and abortion, which probably makes the holocaust look like nothing in comparison to the annihilation of millions of babies today.

Chantal went on to say that they had just finished the first night of the huge all-Filipino musical stage production of *The Lion, The Witch and the Wardrobe* by C.S. Lewis. For this musical production to be approved, they had to submit the whole music and libretto to the C.S. Lewis Foundation in Oxford, England. The man who approved of such productions was Douglas Gresham, the stepson of C.S Lewis.

Douglas Gresham loved the music and the libretto so much that, to surprise the cast, he and his wife Merrie came to Manila to watch the show. It was on one of those nights that he introduced the Hope Alive group counseling therapy module to the whole cast and crew of the theater company. He related how it had helped him and his wife, and invited Chantal or anyone in the company to go to Canada to be trained under Dr. Philip Gordon Ney, founder and president of the International Hope Alive Counselors Association.

Chantal was personally invited by Douglas to train, but she knew at once that she couldn't go and that's why she called me. When I first heard the offer, I flippantly said, "If you raise the money for my fare and if I get a Canadian visa, I will go," thinking that would be close to impossible. In one week, Chantal raised the money for my trip and Doug played a huge part in sending me to Victoria to be trained there for the first time in the Hope Alive Group Counseling training.

That year, I went through the Level I group counseling training, took my exams and got my certificate. After two years, I underwent further training as a supervisor and trainer of this wonderful Christian and scientific counseling module. I have become a member of the International Hope Alive Counselors Association, and Douglas and Merrie Gresham and I have been Hope Alive colleagues since 1999. We would see each other every year at the Hope Alive annual general meetings, which are held mostly in Europe. Since that time, I have met more people from other countries and have traveled to Europe and Africa as part of this great ministry.

Second Miracle Prayer Request: A Trip To Europe

Number two in my first miracle prayer list was a trip to Europe. I said, *"God, I would also like to go on an all-expense-paid trip around Europe if it's okay with you. I also don't like to raise money for it please? Sige na? (Pretty please?)"*

You see the posture of my heart when I pray these prayers is not, "Lord, you owe me," praying with a clenched fist, reminding Him of what I deserved. But the posture of my heart was more like a little girl on her daddy's lap, and so with love and *lambing* (tender affection), I asked, *"Daddy, may I?"*

In the year 2000, I was invited to Poland in Eastern Europe for my first ever Hope Alive International Conference. I traveled with Chantal and another lovely artist friend. I met up with them in London, and we stayed at Middlesex, at the home of a funny, crazy, loving, actor, Junix Inocian and his wife Annie and son Yñaqui. For those who don't know, Junix was one of the original cast of Miss Saigon in London's West End. That was a real fun trip! From London, we flew to Poland with Douglas and Merrie Gresham, who were already my Hope Alive colleagues.

From Poland, after the Hope Alive Conference, everyone including my two artist friends went home, but I had to go explore Europe some more on my own! I hopped on a train to meet friends in Hamburg. It was the kind of train that you see in movies where you sit on a coach facing each other. The coach I got on was empty and because I was so tired I lay down on the three seats with my back toward whoever sat in front of me. Just as I woke up and turned, I saw this gorgeously handsome man sitting in front of me and I died. How embarrassing! I smiled and he smiled back. He had this suave European manly air about him that made me want to reach out a hand to him and blurt out, "Are you Bond? James Bond?" It turned out that he was a Dutch-Italian environmentalist who was passionate about saving the Antarctic. How fun was that?

His personality really fascinated me. I was a very awkward Asian, not knowing where I was, and he was such a gentleman. We struck up a conversation. He pointed out to me where the Berlin wall used to be. When we got off the train, he was so nice as to take me to my next platform. I guess I had a sign on my forehead that said "Lost Filipina." He was such a calm and collected soul that he made me feel safe and protected. Apart from the fact that he was such a handsome man, he was also knowledgeable about stuff. I asked God, "Why can't I bring this man home?!" I love men like these!

I knew God would provide for my fare and conference fees, and I remembered that miracle prayer I made, so I was waiting for my miracle. I didn't know how it would come about or if it was going to happen that year. Then a week before I was to leave for London, one of my artist friends gave me $500 from out of the blue saying she wanted me to have it for my trip. At that time, that amount was enough for me to go on a coach bus tour around Europe, where I took a ferry from the port of Dover in London to the port of Calais, France, then a coach bus through Amsterdam, Belgium, Germany, Luxembourg and back to Paris. That was super cool! It was the first time in my life that I traveled alone, and experienced a day where I had breakfast in Germany, lunch in Luxembourg and dinner in Paris!

Have Faith, Will Travel

I have come to realize that traveling entails a lot of trust. When I travel I always wonder how in the world a huge plane made of tons of steel can go up in the air. I can sit on a plane piloted by a complete stranger who tells me, "Hello, this is your Captain speaking. We will bring you to your destination in ten hours," and actually believe that he'll do as he says. If that's not faith, I don't know what is.

As a missionary, oftentimes I find myself in situations where my life is in the hands of my hosts. When I land in a country, it takes a lot of faith to believe that my host will truly be there to welcome me. When I do see a familiar face on the other side of the welcoming area, my heart rests. Oftentimes, I do not know the host personally or the itinerary that has been prepared for me, or the living conditions in which I will find myself. But I go nonetheless, believing that things will work out fine.

When I enter a new culture, I set my heart to trust people and receive their hospitality. When I trust people and what they offer to me, eventually I entrust my life to Someone bigger. All throughout my journey, trusting has been required of me. I realize that it is God's invitation for me to see my faith in Him grow. Maybe that's why I travel a lot. It sets me up to trust God in a big way.

May I Have A Husband Now?

Somewhere along the way, I asked God, "Okay my dear Lord, inasmuch as marriage doesn't seem anywhere near my horizon at the moment, will You please just allow me to see the whole world?" That was my ex-deal with God. This year I traveled to my 30th country. Today as I am writing this paragraph, I am on top of a sixteen-floor condominium facing the beautiful horizon of Chaam, Long Beach in Thailand. This is the home of my ministry partner. She thought I would love the place and has made it available so I can write my first book.

But today, I told God, *"Okay, enough traveling, God! May I have my husband now?"*

Next on my first miracle prayer list was a brand new car. "God," I pointed out, "You see my old rickety cranky car? This car is 15 years old and I think it wants to retire. It's embarrassing when I meet the ladies for discipleship in hotels and my car screeches, and I get those looks? So may I ask for a nice one? May I ask for a brand new car, please?" Well, I had my first brand new car in 2001 and my second brand new car in 2007 and God used two lovely lady friends of mine to give these gifts! HalleluYAH!

My fourth miracle prayer request was: A rich, handsome, godly husband who will love me well and with whom I can serve Jesus in any way. I made a mistake! Now I agree with all my girlfriends. They said I should have asked for a husband FIRST! God would have granted that prayer and then I would have a husband who had money to travel to the US and Europe and buy me my brand-new car. Hah! What was I thinking?! They're right. I should have done that first!

My Seemingly Impossible Miracle Prayer Request Today

I want to let you in on my seemingly impossible miracle prayer request this year. I'm asking God to stir the heart of one or two individuals to give toward a house and lot in Quezon City, Philippines that has an area of not less than 300 square meters. This will be used as a Hope Alive Manila Center, where men and women who are damaged by abuse, neglect, and abortions can find help, hope and healing. There will be four counseling rooms and an office and the second floor can be a halfway house for pregnant mothers whom we have convinced not to abort their children. Isn't this exciting? Thank you Lord, for this house! If God is stirring your heart to be this person, please call or email me.

Oh, and I still want a rich, godly, handsome husband…!

Journaling my Thoughts

- ★ What are the seemingly impossible things you want to trust God for this year? We have the same God, don't we? Get a pen now and make your own Miracle Prayer List.

- ★ Share this list with two or three godly individuals who can pray and trust God with you for His answers to these requests.

- ★ What exciting, daring, fun event would you want to do before you turn 50 or 60? What countries would you like to see as a single person? Schedule when you want to do this and invite me, okay?

★ Write your prayer to God here.

CHAPTER SEVENTEEN

GFF: Girlfriends Forever!

17 GFFs: Girlfriends Forever!

"Your husband has to be rich because you have friends like us," Chantal remarked during one of the times they blessed me for a husband on my birthday.

Another friend, Christie, lovingly told me to my face, *"Basta, Orpah kung yang lalaking yan mahal ka, kailangan dadalhin nya at papamasahihan nya kaming lahat sa US,"* which means, "If this man really loves you and intends to marry you, he will have to get tickets for all five of us to attend your wedding in the US!"

This was the topic of a conversation I had with these ladies when I came home from the US one fine October day. Five of my beautiful GFFs treated me to a birthday dinner and sat me down so we could discuss this man I dated in the US. Take note, I only told them I was just dating him…

Already they were threatening to decapitate him if he didn't treat me well! If he at any time broke my heart, they would have to deal with him. The poor guy, he hadn't so much as stepped into my country and his life was already in danger.

No wonder I don't have a husband yet!

I laugh about all these now, because you see, I'm privileged to know a handful of women who really love me well. They are the ones I treasure in my heart. With the personality that I have, I keep only a few women friends and these few are the ones I know I can be real with and would love me to bits! I pick one real good girlfriend in every country, too. I have one special friend in each place I've visited: Simone, in

Belgium; Sophie in Arkansas; Veronique in Canada; Brigita in Nigeria; and Margaux in Malta.

We All Need Girl Friends

I love my girlfriends! They are gifts from God! They're a great source of love and wisdom, care, fun and lots of craziness that I need throughout my journey of singleness.

I have old friends; young friends; fat and skinny friends; crazy and serious friends; authentic and way-out-there friends; friends I get to see once a year; friends who live nearby; and friends on the other side of the globe.

However different, unique and crazy these girlfriends are, I know that God has handpicked each of them to help me grow and mature, speak truth to me, rebuke and love me, and keep me grounded.

Yes, they are few, but they are well-chosen friends. Because they know they are my friends, we love to do things together, I can call them anytime, I'm free to invite myself over to their homes, or treat them out to dinner or movies or just about anything that will make them happy. I hold them very close to my heart, and they know this. They also know that I will be the first to rebuke them if I see them doing wrong, because I love them and want the best for them.

What do girlfriends have to offer that boyfriends cannot? For one, they like going to beauty salons with you! Men don't! We can go on and on just talking…actually, they talk a lot more. I guess I'm more like a man that way. I easily get tired when I talk. Sometimes I do have a few words but they're all in my brain. This probably makes me a good listener to my GFFs who like to talk.

I always tell my married GFFs that I take my hat off to them as mothers because I can't imagine living life the way they do. Whether they are stay-at-home or working moms, as soon as they wake up, they need to think of a thousand and one things for their husband and children: for example, what they'll eat not just this morning but for the rest of the day, what the children will need for school, if the helpers have managed things well at home. Only afterwards can they think about themselves or spend quiet time alone. Then there's the extra challenge to stay pretty enough for their husband, or be ready for a romantic night. The list can go on.

But for me, every morning when I wake up, all I think of is my coffee and myself and if my dog has already peed. Am I complaining? Oh no, no, no!

Fiona and Laurence

Fiona, a single, never-married petite lady, came to me one day and said, "I want to be your friend!" With both surprise and delight, I replied, "Well, of course, I'd love to be your friend too!" I have welcomed Fiona into my life since then. She is a lady who loves to serve and give. After a trip, even if it may just be to the next town, Fiona will always have something for me. Birthdays, Christmases, Valentine's Days, and sometimes even when there's no occasion, Fiona never fails to give me something just to tell me she is thinking of me. I am humbled, sometimes ashamed, that I may not be thinking of her as often as she may be thinking of me! I have learned to be thoughtful because of Fiona.

Because friendship is a two way street, I feel that my role in Fiona's life is to protect her from people who take advantage of her kindness. I always have to remind her to say "No" to people and to delegate jobs so she doesn't end up doing everything herself.

Fiona is always the first to ask me if I'm okay during any crisis or whenever she senses something is wrong. Fiona is the best person I go to when I need help because I know she will do anything to help me. I think she will be a fine wife for any man and I've been wondering why she too isn't married yet. Maybe the best compliment about Fiona that I have heard from one good male married friend is this: "If only men knew what they're missing by not being married to you, Fiona, they'd go crazy!" He's right! If I were a man, I'd marry her!

Fiona is so committed to me that she would lovingly tell me, "Orpah, you need to be more kind with your words," or "Orpah, don't do that!" or "Orpah, what did you think was wrong with what you did?" Or "Orpah, did you see how you hurt her?" And after all the excuses and all the ways I'd try to justify my evil deeds, I would know it's the Holy Spirit reminding me through her to repent and be quick about it! Somehow when she speaks like that, I need to listen and I'm glad she does that to me. Thank you, God, for my GFF, Fiona!

Laurence is my running partner, my pelota, or racquetball buddy. She pushes me hard when I'm too lazy to even wake up to meet her for our morning exercise. She finds creative ways just to make me get up from bed. She bribes me to a movie date, cooks breakfasts, and treats me to anything just so I would develop the habit of exercising in the morning. She taught me how to play pelota, which is the Filipino counterpart of racquetball, although pelota makes use of only two sides of the wall instead of four. It is a wonderful game of strength, speed, geometry, and quick thinking.

I would often sense the quality of the relationship of Laurence and her husband whenever we played this game. On very cool, light days and when everything was okay at home, our pelota games would be so leisurely I could beat her in three games. But on days when things got crazy at home and she and her husband had something unsettled between them, Laurence would beat the life out of me and in a very short time it would be "Game Over! You're dead!" Later, I learned to ask first, "Will I die today, Laurence?" and if she said, "Yes!" I knew I'd be in for a torturous, groan-filled three games of pelota! Well, I guess pelota serves as a wonderful way to sweat out all sorts of pent-up emotions for us. There were times when we destroyed some balls on bad days. Now that we are older, she is a little bit more lenient. Now I will have to bribe her to take me out to play anything! I love this lady and I miss her for she has moved to North America. Thank you, Lord, for Laurence!

Isabelle and Francoise

I met Isabelle when I was taking my Master's degree in Biblical Counseling. Because I'm a kinesthetic learner, I would always sit at the back so I could do other things, like snooze, or do my homework, while my teachers took hours and hours teaching. My attention span is very short. If the teacher talked on and on, my capacity to learn would be about filled up in 20 minutes flat. Isabelle was my seatmate and that's how she and I became friends. She would save a chair for me right next to her. She shared a lot with me, uhm…things like, she would bring her manicure set to class and do her nails while the teacher lectured about all the psychopathologic disorders, which to me didn't make sense at all! I'd always smile each time Isabelle removed her cuticles using a cute little thingy. The next thing I knew she had brought me a set of that nice manicure stuff so we could do it together! We would laugh as we pretended to be listening to the teacher while making sure that we had the most manicured pretty fingers by the time we left the room! We were drawn to each other so much that we called ourselves "my Sweetmate!"

We have kept our friendship over the years. Isabelle is sincerely happy when she discovers beautiful things about my life as I struggle toward maturity. She calls my attention to what I may be doing wrong but is also quick to affirm what I am doing right. My Sweetmate is quick to admit that she doesn't have the best marriage. Sometimes she says quite outspokenly how envious she is that I'm single while she's stuck with her husband. Yet she's quick to say that she's thankful for her husband because it's God's way of refining her. One of these days my hope is to bring her along with me to a trip to Montagne d'amour in Canada—just the two of us!—so she can get away temporarily from her hubby and relish just being herself. I love my Sweetmate! Thank you, dear Lord, for my Sweetmate, Isabelle!

Françoise is my partner in life and love! We have the same crushes, same love for food, adventure and music. She is a crazily funny person who loves to laugh and dance and sing even when there's no music around! She and I sometimes go on trips here and outside the country. She is a single mother of three. My relationship with her has evolved from that of discipler-disciple to being co-equals in the faith. Now, I feel I'm learning more from her as she disciples me in the many things she's learning in her walk with Jesus. She's one person who can express herself unashamedly. She worships and sings and praises God so! Because of her, I learn to be unashamed in my worship of Jesus.

When I was starting to write this book, Françoise and I went out on a coffee date. With excitement, I shared with her the concept of my book and how I thought this book would have an impact on many single ladies' lives. But I said I didn't know when I would ever finish this book! Françoise quickly offered encouraging words to me and told me I had to do it. To signify her trust in me and her belief that God has ordained me to write and finish this book, she pulled out her cheque book, wrote a considerable amount to my name, placed it in front of me, and said, "Here's seed money for your book! Use it for whatever you need to finish it!" I squealed with both delight and fear and said, "Oh no, that means I really have to finish this book now!" Thank you, God, for Françoise!

Sabine and Gladys

Sabine and Gladys are my GFFs who I believe have the biggest faith in God and don't know it. They are two of the women I have Bible Studies with. I've watched how they've grown in their Christian faith and in the way they've become better businesswomen. Both of them are producers of events and concerts and have been managers of artists for many years. These two ladies decided a long time ago that each time I led the Bible Study, they would be the ones to choose the restaurant where we would meet, and they would take turns footing the bill. Not a bad deal! So every week, we would go to some five-star hotel or a wonderful fine dining restaurant. Their excuse has always been, "Look, we work hard all week and our only vice is eating in a good restaurant." Who's to argue with that?

I haven't met many women who take risks in their businesses as these women do. Whether they earn from these businesses or not, they always declare that it's a learning experience from God. I like these executive, powerful, authoritative women who are able to do the things they want to do when they want to do it.

One particular lunch date turned out to be quite a unique conversation.

> Sabine: "I'm on my way to New York next week for a medical appointment and I want to watch Lea Salonga on her last week of performance for Miss Saigon on Broadway."
>
> Gladys (teasingly): "Huh? I want to come too! Can I come?"
>
> Sabine: "Sure, why not?

> Then seemingly instinctively and unrehearsed, they both turn toward my direction on cue and ask: "What about you, Orpah? Would you like to come to New York too?" I say to myself, "Yeah right, like I can just hop on a plane next week, right?" I decide to play along instead.
>
> Orpah: "Sure! I would love to come!"
>
> Sabine and Gladys (in unison): "Okay then, lets all go to New York!"

Now, understand that up until that point, I'm thinking that this is all a joke. But the next thing I knew, I had a round trip ticket to LA and New York that same week! We had a lovely time in New York because for the first time both of them had no shows or events to produce and the trip was an easy, relaxing one. Yes, New York can be relaxing for some of us, you know! So off we went to watch Lea Salonga on Broadway. Initially they said they had no more seats, but guess where we ended up? On the fourth row, center aisle, where we could almost see Lea's hard palate when she sang! What a treat that show was! One more Broadway show, "The Lion King", plus New York's best cheesecake and my week was made! Thank you, my dear Lord, for my GFFs Sabine and Gladys!

I can go on and on talking about more of my lady friends. I can tell you all the great and wonderful blessings of having good, married and non-married GFFs. They are worth keeping! Honestly, I am mostly on the receiving end of these relationships. Having GFFs is healthy for my soul. Having GFFs polishes my rough edges, and makes my heart bloom.

So what if there's a man and he's not mine? My GFFs will always be around and they will love me to bits. Thank You, Lord, for all my GFFs!

Journaling my Thoughts

★ Who are your GFFs? What does each of them bring into your friendship?

★ Are they authentic with you? Will they rebuke you in love when you need the correction? Can you name instances when they spoke courageously into your life?

★ What do you bring to their lives that will help them bloom as women? Or are you always on the receiving end?

★ Write a quick note to each of them, sharing how much you appreciate them as your Girlfriends Forever. Send them the cards this week.

★ Write your prayer to God about them here.

Good Ol' Lydia

CHAPTER EIGHTEEN

18 Good Ol' Lydia!

I have been looking at some examples of women in the Bible who were single and lived their lives to the full. Initially, I thought of Ruth after she was widowed and she came to live with her mother-in-law, Naomi, but shortly after she became single, she got married again. I thought of Mary Magdalene, but she didn't quite fit—she had too many men in her life. Then Esther, but she was too ideal…too many milk baths!

Lydia: A Woman Who Changed A City

It was through an online message shared by Dr. Bob Shirock of Oak Pointe Church, Michigan, titled "A Woman Who Changed a City,"[35] where I first fully understood the story of a single woman named Lydia.

I almost identified myself fully with Lydia. If I had known her, we probably would have been good friends! It's quite interesting that there were only two verses dedicated to Lydia, but they say a lot about her. I like that. I like the fact that she may have played a very small part in the New Testament but she made a great impact on the lives of many believers.

Acts 16:14-15 says,

> A woman named Lydia, from the city of Thyatira, a seller of purple fabrics, a worshiper of God, was listening; and the Lord opened her heart to respond to the things spoken by Paul. And when she and her household had been baptized, she urged us, saying,

[35] See the April 3, 2011 Oak Pointe Church podcast under the *Ordinary for Extraordinary Series.* http://oakpointe.libsyn.com/a-woman-who-changed-a-city-4-3-11-audio-podcast.

> "If you have judged me to be faithful to the Lord, come into my house and stay. And she prevailed upon us."

According to Dr. Shirock, Thyatira was a city in Asia Minor, and one of the seven churches addressed by John in the Book of Revelation 1:11 and 2:18. The passage says Lydia was a seller of purple fabrics, which tells us of the kind of business she might have engaged in. Purple fabrics were expensive commodities in the ancient world, and it's quite likely that Lydia dealt with rich, wealthy, and maybe famous customers.

A website on inspirational stories and teaching materials adds the following information:

> Purple cloth in those days was very expensive because it was difficult to make. The dye for the cloth came from a shellfish. The juice was white while it was in the veins of the shellfish, but when it was exposed to the sun, the liquid changed into bright purple and red. It took a lot of work to catch enough shellfish to dye even one garment. The beautiful cloth was mainly used by members of the royal families and Roman senators who were required to have a purple band around the edge of their togas, or robes.[36]

Lydia must have been a very successful businesswoman because she could afford to buy and sell these purple cloths.

I imagine Lydia to be a choleric go-getter with lots of business connections. She may have been her own boss. But notice that, despite her influence, verse 14 says that Lydia "listened" and that she was a worshipper of God. Although she was a busy businesswoman, she was nonetheless a very spiritual one. Some commentators say that she might have been a Gentile woman converted to Judaism since the term "worshippers of the True God" is how Gentiles who believed in Yahweh, the Jewish God, were called. I imagine she was also humble enough to listen to what the apostles were saying. The result? The Lord "opened her heart to respond to the things spoken by Paul." Lydia opened her heart to God and allowed God to speak to her and make Himself known to her.

I have worked with many busy, choleric, wealthy, self-made women who model Lydia to me. These beautiful, godly women sincerely want to

---

[36] Garden of Praise is a free educational website that provides great teaching materials on Bible characters. www.gardenofpraise.com/bibl62s.htm (Last accessed 11/10/2011).

know God, listen to Him, and make themselves available to Him. Like Lydia, they seek to be mightily used by God. When God calls, they say, "Yes, I'm willing!" God then opens their hearts to receive Him.

Many Bible scholars believe Lydia was single. That's why I picked her for this chapter. The Biblical account doesn't say anything about a husband and it sounds like the household was her own. It doesn't say anything about her having to ask permission from a husband if she could invite people to their home. I'm sure that being single may have been difficult in a world where it was a disadvantage for a woman to be without a man in her life. Hmmm…sounds pretty much like the world I'm in today.

I'm amazed that God picked a God-fearing single woman to do something significant for Him at that appointed time. I love the fact that God takes notice of these seemingly insignificant individuals. God in His abundant goodness wants to use single women like you and me who are available for Him—and to use them in amazing ways.

Lydia was also a baptized woman. Can you picture it? Lydia must have said to Paul, "Okay, what else do I need to do? Do you want me to be baptized now? Lets go do it!" Lydia's courage to be identified with the believers of Jesus Christ showed me a sense of urgency to want to be in the center of God's will. In submitting herself to baptism, she was repenting of her sins and turning away from a life apart from God. Now she was entering a new way of life through the acknowledgment of Jesus' death and resurrection. She had opened her heart, professed her faith, and now she wanted the same baptism for her whole family and household.

Lydia must have been a very hospitable woman. She had a home, and I can imagine it must have been a big home because of her business and influence. She probably made sure her home was presentable to her rich clientele. She invited the disciples into her home and offered it as a meeting place for Christian believers. She knew she had something worthy to offer these followers of Jesus, and used her resources in their service. Eventually, her home became the first church, and one of the best churches in Philippi. That is so cool!

The last thing we see about Lydia is that she was persuasive. This version says she "prevailed upon" Paul and his companions. To "prevail" means to "persuade to do something," and I had to laugh because this is where I identify with her the most! I really like Lydia! Paul and his followers may have had other plans about where to stay in Philippi but Lydia convinced them to stay in her house. Verse 15 says, "...she urged us....she prevailed upon us." Of course I can only speculate, but it seems that good ol' Lydia was one persuasive and determined woman! She prevailed, I am sure, in an authentic and non-manipulative way (at least I hope so) to fulfill God's will for her life.

Single Women Can Be Influential

I've always wanted to influence people by being a model of faith to them. God has given me the privilege to work with influential men and women in the arts and entertainment, media and the business sectors of our country. I realize that I'm very much like Lydia: I grab opportunities when I see one, I like using my home to minister to people, and I like to use my resources so that people will be drawn closer to God. I know that I can only take from God whatever amount I open up for Him to fill. When I listen and receive, I am the most blessed of all. I have always asked God to help me live a life that will impact people for good and inspire them to change. I thank God that my unique training in counseling enables me to help bring hope and healing to people's lives. I do this best of all by introducing them to the Source of life and hope, Jesus Christ.

Truly God used Lydia to change the world around her. All she did was to listen, have an open heart and say "Yes" to all the things that she felt God had prompted her to do. God in His goodness and faithfulness made her life fruitful as a single woman. Oh, to be like Lydia!

WHY IS THERE A MAN AND HE'S NOT MINE? Maybe because we still have many things to do that only we as singles can. You and I may be called to be single like Lydia, who in her singleness made a huge impact on her world for God's kingdom. What a wonderful mission, and model, we have!

Journaling my Thoughts

★ How did Lydia's story impact you?

★ How does your life as a single woman impact your world?

★ What do you think will you need to change in your life so that you can become more like Lydia?

★ How would you like your epitaph to read when you've gone to be with Jesus? Write the words here.

★ Write your thoughts and prayers to God here.

Single & Beautiful, For Better or For Worse!

CHAPTER NINETEEN

19 Single & Beautiful, For Better or For Worse!

I have to congratulate you for getting this far in my book. This has been one crazy, difficult, but hopefully truthful, journey. I must be nuts to expose my life so and bare my soul to readers I do not know! But I figured, if I didn't do it now, I never would. Besides, who else would be insane enough to do this?

I just want to say to all of you singles out there that I'm with you. I hear you and I struggle with you. It's a daily thing. Yes, it is hard to be single in a couples' world, but we have the capacity to live beautifully with a heart that is truly alive. It's going to be quite a struggle to stay single and pure. But it can be done in the power of the Holy Spirit.

I do have deep joy amid moments of loneliness. I do offer hope because in Jesus we have hope. I do give my heart in relationships with men and women and I nurture them. We grow in our relationships with each other.

Just like the words of the song "For Good," from the musical *Wicked,* I want people who come into relationship with me to be changed for good. Look at the words from some parts of the song:

> I've heard it said
> That people come into our lives for a reason
> Bringing something we must learn
> And we are led to those who help us most to grow
> If we let them and we help them in return
> Well, I don't know if I believe that's true
> But I know I'm who I am today
> Because I knew you...
> Like a comet pulled from orbit as it passes a sun

Like a stream that meets a boulder
Halfway through the woods
Who can say if I've been changed for the better?
But because I knew you I have been changed for good…[37]

I made a resolve a few years back that whether or not there was a man in my life, I would still be a beautiful, fun-loving, adventurous, connected single woman who loves Jesus and continues to walk with Him. For better or for worse, I will trust in God to fill all the longings of my heart. For better or for worse, I will rest my heart in the goodness of God who knows what is best for me. For better or for worse, I will live well with a heart that is alive and ready to give and receive.

Who knows? I might still get married! That would be great! I haven't given up looking nor have I stopped asking. For all we know, I might write another book next year with a title that says, "Here Is The Man and He's Mine!" Or I may never get married. I believe that, right now, I can truly say with all my heart that I am okay with that too, if that is really God's design for me.

Whatever God chooses for my life from here on, I have made a choice that I will live, love and serve my Jesus. I will wait on Him. I will rest in His goodness and expect more miracles from Him.

When I die, I want these words as my epitaph:

Here lies Orpah Omega Lee who lived her life to the hilt! She was one of the best single ladies in town. She helped many people to know Jesus as their personal Savior and Lord. She had an amazing impact on the lives of men and women who changed their lives because of her influence and now enjoy deep walks with Jesus. She's crazy and fun Auntie Pah to her nephews and nieces who loved her. She's Pingsky to her siblings. She's Orps to the artists in Manila. She traveled the world and had meaningful connections with people. She will be missed. BUT she will not miss you because she is now in the presence of JESUS, her one and only FRIEND, LOVER and HUSBAND!

My dear single and beautiful friend, may God bless, enrich, nourish, give rest to your heart and soul, and manifest to you more of His inexhaustible love and grace.

Orpah Omega Lee

---

[37] Stephen Schwartz, "For Good", from the musical *Wicked*, 2003, http://m.metrolyrics.com/for-good-lyrics-wicked.html.

Journaling my Thoughts

- ★ List down 10-20 single women to whom you would like to give this book to. Make plans on how to send your gift to them this week.

- ★ Please write me an email and let me know your feedback on this book. You can share how it has helped you, or comment on anything that you feel would be important for me to know.

  Send it to: **singlerestedheart@gmail.com**

Appendix

APPENDIX A

Dynamics Of Adultery In The Christian Community

By Dr. Orpah Omega Lee C. Marasigan

A Paper Submitted In Partial Fulfillment Of The Requirements For Psychopathology I, Masters in Biblical Counseling, Alliance Biblical Seminary Quezon City, Philippines November, 1995

I have found out that in our local churches today, we hear of men and women coming before the congregation and confess of sexual immorality while they were in the ministry. These may or may not be leaders in the ministry, but nonetheless, these are the people we thought were the more "godly" ones.

A survey was done by Leadership Journal and it does suggest that we do have a problem in the Christian community. They mailed nearly one thousand letters to pastors and non-pastors and approximately 33 percent of pastors and 45 percent non-pastors had confessed to sexually inappropriate behavior other than their spouse. Another 18 percent of pastors and 28 percent non-pastors admitted to "other forms of sexual contact other than their spouse, i.e., passionate kissing, fondling and mutual masturbation" while in the ministry. 12 percent of pastors since they have been in local-church ministry and 23 percent non-pastors acknowledged having had sexual intercourse with anyone other than their spouse. And of all the others who did not, many indicated their purity had not come easily. ("How Common is Pastoral Indiscretion", p.12)

Why are affairs that attractive to people? Why will a man or a woman who is serving God for many years, be willing to throw away all their investment in the work of God for adulterous relationships? In the same way, why would a beautiful godly single woman throw away all the sweet fruitful devotion to Jesus in exchange for a married man?

I will attempt to show what goes on in the heart and mind of a person as she enters into an adulterous relationship; where it develops slowly and gradually. Maybe this will show us how to help that person make a choice to get out of it or not even go into it.

Some of the Christians I work with, single or married, when asked why they entered into affairs before would tell me statements like: "I was not happy with my spouse anymore;" or "I felt like this man really loved me" or "He made me feel alive!" and "I don't know why, it just happened!" One lady said, "I was single then, and I was getting old, I just had to say yes to him". Most of them would agree that they knew that what they were doing was wrong but at that point, being wrong did not matter.

Many times adultery is experienced by individuals who feel they have missed out on many things in their lives. Adulterous men and women would always justify that they deserve to be happy and would be willing to violate so many other relationships just to enjoy this one.

"We have a right to be happy, don't we? Anything this good has to be right. I would rather go to hell with her than to heaven with my wife." (Petersen, p.3) Quotes like these are what we hear from them.

According to Carder, people who are thinking of having affairs are maybe those feeling ashamed, overwhelmed, unheard, uncared for, possibly trapped, exhausted, numb. Some are disappointed and angry at their spouse's failure to meet their needs. They feel isolated. They feel dead and wonder if they have any passions left. Everything for them is a duty, and a drag. (Carder, p.46)

In one woman's case, she longs for her husband to care more or want her more. For a husband, he may feel that many of his needs are not met by his wife. To singles, friends or family relationships may not be meeting many of their intimacy needs so that any relationship that offers deep friendship and sharing of soul and heart would be such an attraction to them.

"An affair usually begins as a friendship. Usually, the lover is the couple's "best friend" or someone from the spouse's family, or someone in the workplace." (Harley, "How Does an Affair Begin", p.28)

The next thing you know, you look forward to seeing him again, you catch him taking a quick look at you. Then later on, you tell yourself you like this guy but he's married. You observe that he is not enjoying his wife, but he enjoys you.

The real danger comes when the man actually tells you that he likes you and both of you confirm the feeling. It is also at this point that you cry out for help. In many ways, you give hints to Christians around you that you are beginning to fall for this man.

"If you know somebody who is going through this, this might be the most crucial time we need to lovingly disrupt and expose truth to her and help her get out while she still can. Disruption will always have to involve having her speak the truth about it to her husband, or speaking to the man to stop it, or having to flee from him or letting the wife know about her feelings or all of the above. I believe this is only possible if the person sincerely wants out of the relationship, because no matter what noise we do, they will not stop unless they want to.

There was one time when a good, married Christian lady asked to meet with me and in tears she told her story about the battle in her soul because she knows she is enjoying the attention and slowly falling in love with this Christian married man who has obviously seen and may be using her vulnerability. He was relating with her in the guise of encouraging her as a Christian sister. I lovingly told her "Please tell your husband about this soon… today!... otherwise, I will be the one to tell him."

There is always a point where the individual makes a choice. A movie that shows this full well is "Unfaithful". Here is Diane Lane in a phone booth, torn in her heart whether she will go for the urgent pleasure in her soul for a man to satisfy the deep longing right there and now OR walk away and go home to her husband. She decided to go and satisfy her urgent pleasure and as a result, it was an end to a family she has loved, her marriage crumbled, her husband knew about the affair and killed her lover and she was left all alone.

A woman is faced with a tension-filled point of struggle to either give in or hold on to whatever sense of being right is left in her heart. But usually, being right is clouded with wanting to get what she wants…now!

A man in ministry wrote about his battle with lust and the war that continues on in his soul. He was only able to get out when after being exhausted with his double lifestyle, he had enough guts to speak to his wife about it and that was the only time healing started. (see "The War Within". Leadership p.24)

For a woman, an affair is so attractive because she feels she is pursued and wanted and this man will be willing to violate all other relationships just for her. It also gives her a certain illusion of being the one to save him from a terrible relationship. That really feels good for some. Especially if we come from backgrounds of neglect in our family, having had no good intimate relationship with a good godly father who relates with you and blossoms your femininity will cause us always to settle for this one distorted relationship rather than having none.

At some point in her struggle, she demands she has to get what she wants now after suffering for such a long time. The choice may seem like she will commit suicide. It will seem like death to her values in life, death to all her other significant relationships and death to her self-worth, but all these are not apparent to her at this point or she refuses to see it.

Larry Crabb explains this as an issue of demandingness.

Unrelenting pain is a most suitable environment in which to grow a demanding spirit...To insist on something, we must first persuade ourself that what we are after is deserved and legitimate, that we have a solid basis for our demand. And nothing persuades us more completely that our weary soul deserves a break than continued heartache. After years of a thoughtless, non-communicative husband, a wife may come to believe that demanding a better companion is entirely justified. The line between legitimate desiring and illegitimate demanding is thin and easily crossed". (Crabb, p.141)

Men and women cross this line wanting immediate fulfillment of their desires at the expense of many violations they do to themselves and the people they love. Actually, one knows when they have crossed the line.

The married man and the single woman at this point make a decision to keep all these things a secret from people, especially from his wife.

"The first breaking of faith—basic infidelity—precedes any act of extramarital intercourse. It happens when one partner decides to turn away from his mate in search for intimacy or fulfillment and keeps the decision a secret. This is the true betrayal of trust. A man cannot and will not talk to his wife about matters that concerns him deeply and then discusses these concerns with another woman whose company he enjoys. He must keep the relationship a secret because it would wound his wife to know the truth and this in turn reinforces the separation." (Petersen, p.12)

For the single woman, we give hints to our girlfriends and we share about this married man. You see, as the girlfriend we are horrified that she is even talking about this. When we comment about it and say she should get out of the relationship, we soon find out we don't see her anymore for weeks, for months, she turns off her phone and you'll no longer see her.

So what does one girlfriend do? I believe that no matter what we do and what we say, unless the Spirit of God acts and convicts her of the sin and actually pulls her out, she will not be able to get out of that relationship, especially if it has been a sexual relationship.

Dr. Philip Ney has introduced a concept called Pair Bonding. He explains in his HOPE ALIVE GROUP COUNSELING.

"The Bible clearly states that the two shall become one flesh (Genesis 2:22-24; Matthew 19:4-6). They do not become one mind or one spirit. There are no marriages in Heaven (Matthew 22:29-30). God encourages us to maintain our individuality. Vows of commitment, blessings by pastors and priests and witnesses of the commitment are very important, but the essence of marriage is that they become one flesh. In almost every culture or religion, they are married only when and if they have heterosexual intercourse. God marries people and only death breaks that marriage. It is His prerogative and responsibility. Humans cannot make or pronounce others to be married, even if they think they are endowed with that capacity by church or state.

As designed in humans, commitment and bonding should go together in a whole series of situations; first in marriage, then in having children, then in work and then in difficult tasks…

There is evidence that during intercourse the rich mix of hormones in male seminal plasma, e.g. estrone, estradial, testosterone, thyroid stimulating hormone and prostaglandins, are rapidly absorbed in the woman's vagina by an active transport mechanism. The intravaginal absorption of male generated hormones and their possible effect on female behaviour. Medical Hypotheses, 20, 221-231). In this way, she takes on her husband's hormonal profile. There may be a similar mechanism whereby the stratified squamous epithelium of the male's penis absorbs female hormones secreted by the vagina. Hormonally the two truly become one flesh." (Ney, P.G. (1986)

It will be very hard to get a girlfriend out of a relationship especially if she has slept with the man. BUT there is still hope. It almost always has to come to a point when I pray, "Father, set my girlfriend up in a way that she can be able to get out of this relationship as soon as possible. If it has to take the wife finding out and creating a scene, or if it has to take the man to get tired of her, please do it," I actually pray the prayer of Hosea in Hosea 1:6-7 "Therefore, behold, I will hedge up thy way with thorns, and make a wall, that she shall not find her paths. And she shall follow after her lovers, but she shall not overtake them; and she shall seek them, but shall not find them: then shall she say, I will go and return to my first husband; for then was it better with me than now".

I pray to God to either make her so sick of what she is doing or the man in her life will lose interest in her so that she will go back to her true Lover, Jesus Christ!

So the main idea is to expose these relationships, and expose the lies. You see, during the time that both of them decide to go on and keep this a secret between them, sexual intimacy is just inevitable. Having to hide and lie all the time are all a part of the big game.

I believe it is safe to say that all affairs are just manifestations of a deeper problem lying in the heart of the individual.

Adultery, like how Schaumburg speaks about sexual addiction is very much the same.

Sexual addiction is not just an issue of sex or even of external behavior. It is a by-product of loneliness, pain, the self-centered demand to be loved and accepted regardless of the consequences and a loss of vital relationship with God. It primarily stems from the sinfulness of a human heart and a reluctance to be in a passionate, dependent relationship with God. (Schaumburg, p.21)

People want relationships and intimacy that would most satisfy their deepest longings of love and acceptance. People do not go to God and ask God to help them tolerate the fact that they can never be loved and accepted the way they want to, so they look to any relationship that is available and cling on to it. (Jeremiah 2:13) It does not matter who will be violated, nor does it matter how the other person looks, as long as she is wanted in the relationship.

One woman was quoted saying this about her lover. "When I first met him, he repulsed me, but he talked kindly and understandingly; he accepted me, made me feel like a woman-important, attractive and gave me the emotional support I wanted so much from my husband. I ultimately forgot what he looked like, because when someone does this for you, you want to give him back so much more—everything you have". (Petersen, p.5)

We sincerely doubt that our situations are going to ever change for the better and we don't know if God is going to give us the best for us, that's why we settle for anything that would make us feel and experience something good, even for just a moment.

When Christians fall into sexual immorality, a whole gamut of emotions flood the Christians around them. Most of the time we deal with it in anger towards the persons involved. Oftentimes, it feels like there was someone who died when news like these come and the whole community grieves. Sometimes we just totally ignore them, basically because we do not know how to deal with them and having to deal with them will require so much from us.

Some years ago, the news about a famous gospel singer, Michael English, who admitted to an affair with another married singer of First Call, Marabeth Jordan, (see <u>Christianity Today</u>, June 1994, p.64) created so much anger and grief from people who loved his music. Michael English said that he will not return to Christian music anytime in the near future. He has then gone back to secular music and launched a new singing career. (see Christianity Today. Dec. 1994 p.56) What a loss that was to the whole community then.

Adultery requires such a big price to the individual himself, to his spouse, to his children, and to his church. I believe that any Christian's or a minister's work will never be the same.

In the book, "If Ministers Fall, Can They Be Restored?", a minister who falls into adultery has to deal with the fact that they will always get into the cycle of sorrow, shame and grief. "Most painful for them is knowing they have betrayed the Lord." (LaHaye, p.18)

A minister who has had sexual affairs not only faces guilt and loss of self-respect, but he also loses the respect of his congregation. He is never quite sure that his friends aren't viewing him with contempt... All the credit and esteem he enjoyed as an active pastor has vanished. (Ibid., p.21)

This is true of all of Christians because we represent Christ in the whole community especially among unbelievers. Many unbelievers have more reason to mock God because of our choices.

It is a shattering experience for a minister's wife once she knows about the affair—the whole dynamics of shock, grief, anger, loss of ministry, being uprooted, etc. are what she has to face. It is harder because she has to minister to the children while she's grieving and do a lot of explaining to family members and other friends.

Many children are driven to rebellion toward God because of adultery and usually they would do this to spite their fathers. Christian children have to suffer a sudden change from being so respected as a minister's child to feeling so ashamed that he is one.

Some rebellious minister's kids are known to use their father's sin as an excuse to be angry with God. Although they must know that their parents have devoutly prayed that their children would choose to walk in truth, they rebel against God. One of the current leaders of an anti-Christian organization is the angry son of a fallen minister. (Ibid. p.29)

They usually go and do the same thing their father did much like what the Bible says about the sins of their fathers visiting from third to fourth generation. (Exodus 34:7)

But it isn't just the children who suffer...infidelity produces enough hurt to flood the extended family, particularly the minister's parents and parents-in-law. Most ministers' parents are very proud of the fact that their son is a pastor. This pleasure is dashed to pieces when they learn of their son' fall into disgrace. The extent of the pain caused by this one sin is incredible. I can't think of a single family member that is not affected. (Ibid. p.30)

To a single woman, shame, confusion, fear and chaos is in her soul that she thinks her life is now a waste.

Adultery is and never will be a private sin. God has His ways of finding us out. It is more destructive than we think, considering all the effects it will have in you and your family, including the church, the work and the name of Christ.

People who are in these relationships can still get out, and there is hope of healing, but never without consequences. BUT I would rather go through this and be back in my relationship with God rather than stay in a relationship that I know does not honor God and man. People who are exposed to these situations should not be caught unaware of the subtlety of the sin and the gravity of it.

BIBLIOGRAPHY

Carder, Dave. Torn Asunder, Chicago; Moody Press, 1992

Crabb, Larry. Inside Out, Colorado Springs, CO: Navpress, 1988

Harley, Williard F. "How Does an Affair Begin" Worldwide Challenge Magazine. November/December 1989, Vol. 16, No.6 p.28

LaHaye, Tim. "If Ministers Fall Can they be Restored?" Grand Rapids Michigan, Zondervan, 1990

Ney, Phiip G. Hope Alive Manual British Columbia, Pioneer Publishing, 1998

Perkins, Bill. "Fatal Attraction" Eugene, OR: Harvest House Publishers,1991

Petersen, J. Allan. The Myth of the Greener Grass, Wheaton, IL: Tyndale House Publishers 1991

Schaumburg, Harry. False Intimacy, Colorado Springs, CO: Navpress 1992

"Adultery Muzzles Carreers of Singer" Christianity Today, June 20,1994, Vol 38, p.64

"English Launches Second Career" Christianity Today, December 12, 1994 Vol 38, p.56

"The War Within: An Anatomy of Lust" Leadership Journal, Fall, 1982 Vol III, No.4 pp 30-48

"The War Within Continues" Leadership Journal, Winter 1988 Vol X, No.1 pp.24-33

APPENDIX B

How to Know God Personally

By Dr. Bill Bright

What does it take to begin a relationship with God? Devote yourself to unselfish religious deeds? Become a better person so that God will accept you? You may be surprised that none of those things will work. But God has made it very clear in the Bible how we can know Him.

The following principles will explain how you can personally begin a relationship with God, right now, through Jesus Christ...

Principle 1: God loves you and offers a wonderful plan for your life.

God's Love

> "God so loved the world that He gave His one and only Son, that whoever believes in Him shall not perish, but have eternal life." [1]

God's Plan

> [Christ speaking] "I came that they might have life, and might have it abundantly" [that it might be full and meaningful]. [2]

Why is it that most people are not experiencing the abundant life? Because...

Principle 2: All of us sin and our sin has separated us from God.

We Are Sinful

> "All have sinned and fall short of the glory of God." [3]

We were created to have fellowship with God; but, because of our stubborn self-will, we chose to go our own independent way, and fellowship with God was broken. This self-will, characterized by an attitude of active rebellion or passive indifference, is evidence of what the Bible calls sin.

We Are Separated

"The wages of sin is death" [spiritual separation from God]. [4]

This diagram illustrates that God is holy and people are sinful. A great gulf separates us. The arrows illustrate that we are continually trying to reach God and the abundant life through our own efforts, such as a good life, philosophy, or religion—but we inevitably fail.

The third law explains the only way to bridge this gulf...

Principle 3: Jesus Christ is God's only provision for our sin. Through Him we can know and experience God's love and plan for our life.

He Died in Our Place

"God demonstrates His own love toward us, in that while we were yet sinners, Christ died for us." [5]

He Rose From the Dead

"Christ died for our sins...He was buried...He was raised on the third day, according to the Scriptures...He appeared to Peter, then to the twelve. After that He appeared to more than five hundred..."[6]

He Is the Only Way to God

> "Jesus said to him, 'I am the way, and the truth, and the life; no one comes to the Father, but through Me.'" [7]

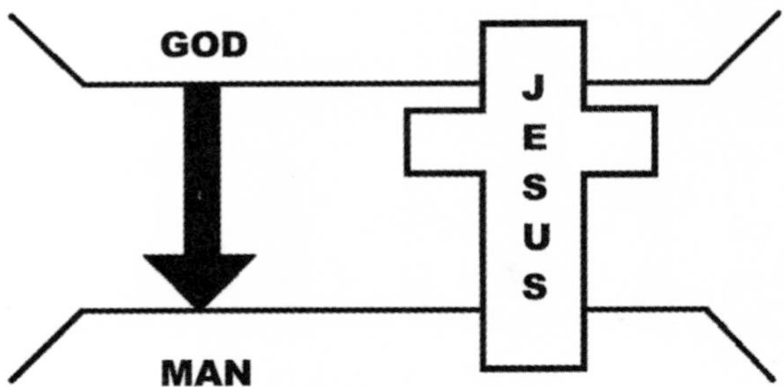

This diagram illustrates that God has bridged the gulf which separates us from Him by sending His Son, Jesus Christ, to die on the cross in our place to pay the penalty for our sins.

It is not enough just to know these three principles...

Principle 4: We must individually receive Jesus Christ as Savior and Lord; then we can know and experience God's love and plan for our lives.

We Must Receive Christ

> "As many as received Him, to them He gave the right to become children of God, even to those who believe in His name." [8]

We Receive Christ Through Faith

> "By grace you have been saved through faith; and that not of yourselves, it is the gift of God; not as a result of works, that no one should boast." [9]

When We Receive Christ, We Experience a New Birth

We Receive Christ by Personal Invitation

> [Christ speaking] "Behold, I stand at the door and knock; if any one hears My voice and opens the door, I will come in to him."[10]

Receiving Christ involves turning to God from self (repentance) and trusting Christ to come into our lives to forgive our sins and to make us what He wants us to be. Just to agree intellectually that Jesus Christ is the Son of God and that He died on the cross for your sins is not enough. Nor is it enough to have an emotional experience. You receive Jesus Christ by faith, as an act of the will.

These two circles represent two kinds of lives:

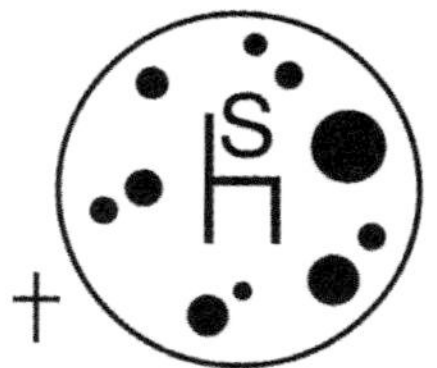

SELF-DIRECTED LIFE
The life of this person is directed by himself. Jesus Christ is not in his life. He always leads his life by his interests. There is always conflict with God's plan.

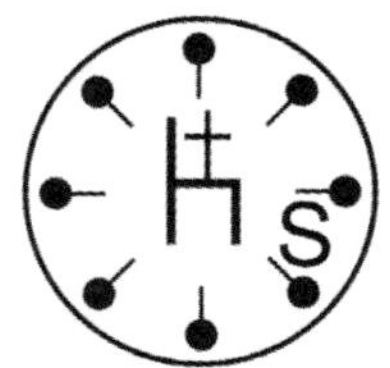

CHRIST-DIRECTED LIFE
The life of this person is directed by Jesus Christ. Jesus Christ is always in his life. He allows Jesus Christ to lead his life. There is peace with God.

Which circle best describes your life?
Which circle would you like to have represent your life?

The following explains how you can receive Christ:

You can receive Christ right now by faith through prayer

Prayer is talking to God. God knows your heart and is not so concerned with your words as He is with the attitude of your heart. The following is a suggested prayer:

> "Lord Jesus, I need You. Thank You for dying on the cross for my sins. I open the door of my life and receive You as my Savior and Lord. Thank You for forgiving my sins and giving me eternal life. Take control of the throne of my life. Make me the kind of person You want me to be."

If this prayer expresses the desire of your heart, then you can pray this prayer right now and Christ will come into your life, as He promised.

Does this prayer express the desire of your heart?

If it does, pray this Prayer right now and Christ will come into your life as He promised.

(1) John 3:16 (NIV); (2) John 10:10; (3) Romans 3:23; (4) Romans 6:23; (5) Romans 5:8; (6) 1 Corinthians 15:3-6; (7) John 14:6; (8) John 1:12; (9) Ephesians 2:8,9; (10) Revelation 3:20

Adapted from Have You Heard of the Four Spiritual Laws and Would You Like to Know God Personally, by Dr. Bill Bright, co-founder of Campus Crusade for Christ.